SWITCHBACKS

David Rox

SWITCHBACKS

Traveling God's Zig-Zag Path to Our Destination

David Rox

BOOKS

Switchbacks: Traveling God's Zig-Zag Path to our Destination by David Rox
Copyright © 2023 by David Rox
All Rights Reserved.
ISBN: 978-1-59755-745-0

Published by: ADVANTAGE BOOKS™, Longwood, FL
www.advbookstore.com

Switchbacks: Traveling God's Zig-Zag Path to our Destination, and parts thereof may not be reproduced in any form, stored in a retrieval system or transmitted in any form by any means (electronic, mechanical, photocopy, recording or otherwise) without prior written permission of the author, except as provided by United States of America copyright law.

Unless otherwise noted, all Scriptural references are from: THE HOLY BIBLE, NEW INTERNATIONAL VERSION®, NIV® Copyright © 1973, 1978, 1984, 2011 by Biblica, Inc.™ Used by permission. All rights reserved worldwide.

Library of Congress Catalog Number: 2023948333

Name:	Rox, David, Author
Title:	*Switchbacks: Traveling God's Zig-Zag Path to our Destination*
	David Rox
	Advantage Books, 2023
Identifiers:	ISBN Paperback: 9781597557450, eBook: 9781597557573
Subjects:	RELIGION: Christian Life – Inspirational

Cover Art Design by Margot Rox

First Printing: December 2023
23 24 25 26 27 28   10 9 8 7 6 5 4 3 2 1

Acknowledgements

Special thanks to my life-long partner, my wife Margot, for making sure this book can be read and enjoyed by women as well as men. Also, a special thanks to Dr. Marvin Wilson for his patient proofreading and helpful input. What wonderful gifts God gives!

Thanks also to all my brothers and sisters at the First Congregational Church of Hamilton, MA, for their input when this material was being taught in an adult Sunday School class. May the Lord bless our efforts and use His Word to further His Kingdom!

Table of Contents

Acknowledgements 5
Introduction 7
1: A Journey To A Miracle: ABRAHAM 9
2: The Rugged Road: JACOB 21
3: Traversing Highs And Lows: JOSEPH 33
4: Falling Off A Cliff: JOB 47
5: The Wilderness Way: MOSES 61
6: A Trail Back Home: RUTH AND NAOMI 77
7: The Long Road To A Crown: DAVID 85
8: A Tale Of Two Mountains: ELIJAH 109
9: Walking With Courage: DANIEL 123
10: A Path To Ponder: MARY 137
11: Coming To The Crossroads: PAUL 151
12: The Purposeful Journey: JESUS 169
13: Switchbacks: FOR YOU AND ME 181
Notes 195
About The Author 197

Introduction

What do I expect from God? Why do I expect it? If I am really honest with myself, do I expect an easy life – a straight path on level ground at all times? Do I live as if I am entitled to an easy time of it? Where did I get this idea from, anyway? Shouldn't my expectations be guided by the Scriptures, where I can see how God has worked in the lives of people down through the ages?

There is a "stream" running through Scripture pointing to the way God often works out His plan. To be sure, we learn in the Bible about who God is, who we are as fallen beings, and what God's plan of salvation is for humankind. But we also learn about *God's process* – how He works out His plan. These biblical stories may give us guidance about how God may be at work in our own lives.

In my many years walking as a Christian, I have discovered that God rarely gives me straight paths to travel. How exasperating! While it is true in geometry that the shortest distance between two points is a straight line (and we often want to travel the shortest distance to save precious time), God does not seem to care about time or distance. He transcends both of them.

It may help to talk about *switchbacks*. A switchback is a zig-zag trail up a mountain. They are designed to make hiking easier. Trying to hike straight up a tall mountain is nigh unto impossible. But trail makers often construct switchbacks that zig-zag up the mountain allowing hikers to climb slowly but surely to the summit. I believe God invented switchbacks. The evidence in Scripture points to the fact that God's process includes more winding trails than straight paths.

The Bible is replete with biographies of people whose lives were bereft of straight paths. This must have been extremely frustrating for some of them. I know it would have been for me. I am a pragmatist – a doer. I love the shortest distance between two points – a straight line. I love tying up all the loose ends quickly and neatly. I am tempted to plow through anything and anyone to get where I want to go in the quickest way. My wife often scolds me (rightly so) for being in "do mode" when I really don't need to be – like at 3:00 AM when I cannot sleep. Few goals are reached by trying to blaze straight trails at that hour in the morning.

As I examined the lives of the Biblical figures discussed in these pages, I couldn't help but notice at times as they traveled towards God's promised goal, they seemed to be going in the opposite direction. Why does God send them north when their ultimate goal is to go south? Being an all-wise and all-knowing God, I am sure He has His reasons.

So, what can be gained from understanding this trait of our loving Creator to put "switchbacks" in our journeys?

- We may learn how God views time as it unfolds in our lives.
- We may come to see ourselves enrolled in a "school of faith" with the Lord as our teacher.
- We can gain insight as to how He might want his Kingdom and Gospel to spread – according to his timetable and direction rather than our own.
- We might begin to see how God answers our prayers in the most roundabout ways.
- We might even discover how God can use guilt-ridden failure in our lives to work out His purposes.
- We can learn to combat our "straight path" mindset with Biblical faith and hope.

Now don't get me wrong. I am not saying God never provides straight pathways in our lives. He does from time to time, and He certainly can do whatever He chooses to do. When examining biblical narrative – the life stories of people in the Bible – we can often make the mistake of assuming that what happened to them will happen to us. We should never make that mistake! For example, when Balaam's donkey spoke the word of the Lord to him (Numbers 22:21ff), that does not mean donkeys are going to speak to us! However, there is plenty of evidence to support these two statements made by the prophet Isaiah – one a clear reminder of reality and the other a divine invitation:

"For my thoughts are not your thoughts, neither are your ways my ways, declares the LORD." (Isaiah 55:8)

Come now, let us reason together, says the LORD . . . ." (Isaiah 1:18a)

So, let's get started.

Switchbacks

1

A Journey to a Miracle: ABRAHAM

"Why does history take such a long, long time – when your waiting for a miracle?"
song lyrics by Bruce Cockburn, *Waiting for a Miracle*

One of the most frustrating things that can happen is going to a fast food restaurant and having to wait a long time for your food. I once left a Burger King in disgust after waiting 20 minutes for food that never came. Fast food? Not that day!

Have you ever waited 24 years for a promise to be fulfilled? Abraham did. I am not sure he was always patient, but he is called a man of faith and the friend of God. The story of Abram (or Abraham, as he was later named) is a familiar one to many of us, Let's look briefly at his life and see how many "straight paths" we can find.

Background

In Genesis Chapter 11 we are given some background information about Abram's family history. Abram's father was Terah. He was a moon worshipper in Ur of the Chaldeans. Abram was the oldest of at least three sons. Son #3 (Haran) died in the land he was born – in Ur. This was the usual place to die in those days – where you were born. Haran left a son Lot, Abram's nephew. Abram had a wife Sarai, and no children. Abram's other brother Nahor married Lot's sister, his niece, and had two daughters. Years later, Nahor had a granddaughter named Rebekah, who entered the biblical narrative in the next generation in the book of Genesis.

Terah set out for Canaan with Lot and Abram – his goal was the land of Canaan but he only got as far as a town called Haran. Abram's father died in Haran – never completing his life's goal of getting to Canaan.

What was Abram, now seventy-five years old and childless, going to do? The story begins in Genesis 12.

Leave and Follow

God made the first move. He called Abram and initiated a relationship. He is always the initiator in Scripture, but this particular call changes the history of the entire world.

> *The LORD said to Abram, "Leave your country, your people and your father's household and go to a land I will show you. I will make you into a great nation and I will bless you; I will make your name great, and you will be a blessing. I will bless those who bless you, and whoever curses you I will curse; and all peoples on earth will be blessed through you." (Genesis 12:1-3)*

As far as we know, Abram knew little about this God who was calling him. And as we shall see, God knew Abram had a lot of learning to do. The first thing Abram had to do was to leave what was familiar. Moving to a new location was risky, especially in the ancient world. When a parent dies, we may make hasty, poor decisions because of our grief. Might Abram have had second thoughts at this point? All his security and desire for self-preservation would be tossed to the wind. Would this be a prudent move?

The next thing he was told to do was to follow God's leading. "Go to a place I will show you." Would you follow someone you don't know well? Remember, Abram didn't have centuries of Scriptural history to rely upon yet! I would be extremely reticent. God promised to show him where to go, but did not give him any details. It turned out that God sent him into the land of Canaan, where his father Terah had dreamed of going. But there was no hint of this yet.

Leave and follow. God said it to Abram, and God's Son later said it to his would-be disciples. *"Come, follow me," Jesus said, "and I will send you out to fish for people." At once they left their nets and followed him.* (Matthew 4:19-20)

There are times in our lives when God says the same thing to us: "Leave and follow." Does it make sense? Not always.

God Made Promises

Then God started promising Abram wonderful things – all in accordance with his divine plan to save the world from sin. Look at the list of promises. What generosity! If Abram agreed to obey God's call to "leave and follow," God would make him into a great nation, he would receive spiritual (and material) blessings, his name would be famous, and others would be blessed because of him. On top of all this, God promised to protect Abram by blessing those who bless him and cursing those who curse him.

This sounds almost too good to be true. Do you suppose Abram had questions? The first that comes to mind is how can God make him into a great nation? He doesn't even have a child yet at the ripe old age of seventy-five.

But all in all, it sounded like a promise worth pursuing. In faith, Abram obeyed and went. What he had accumulated and acquired he brought with him. He also brought his nephew Lot and his entourage with him, even though God had told him to leave his people and his father's household. Might Lot's coming along been Abram's insurance policy in case difficulties arose? Was Abram bringing along a "plan B" just in case he needed one? Was he being a *trifle* disobedient? The Scriptural account is not clear, but bringing Lot with him complicated things down the road, as we shall see.

Off to Canaan

Abram left Haran and entered the land of Canaan. He traveled through the land as far as Shechem. (Genesis 12:6) He noticed the land was occupied by Canaanites. The land was thickly settled and not for sale to a nomadic outsider.

Then the Lord appeared to him a second time while in Shechem, and in one short sentence made two generous promises. *"I will give your offspring this land."* (Genesis 12:7) These promises – offspring and land for them – clarified God's first promises to him, and may be the reason he decided to build an altar there to the Lord. What might have been going on in his mind while worshipping at that altar? Abram might have said: *"God used the 'O' word – offspring! And my kids are going to possess this land!"*

Abram had been waiting for quite a while already for a son and heir. After all, this was the only way God's promises could come true. He had also walked through land God promised his offspring. Meanwhile he had received promises of God's provision, protection and blessing. His hopes had to be high and the future looked bright indeed. His choice to build altars and worship his new-found God were evidence that he was believing and trusting God. It looked like God's straight path for Abram's life was about to unfold.

Famine and Egypt

We might expect at this point that Sarai would get pregnant and have a son. Not yet! Instead, things got tougher for Abram. There was a famine in Canaan. This was life-threatening. It was not like going to the super market and finding out they do not have any toilet paper. Abram had to go to Egypt as a refugee – into a land he had not been promised and fraught with perils, even for a fairly wealthy nomad.

Let's pause for a moment and reflect upon this seeming "detour" in the life of Abram. Why would God promise Canaan and deliver Egypt instead? What has Egypt got to do with the promises of God? We often ask ourselves questions like this. What does my current experience have to do with what I expect from God? Many times God's plan and promises to us clash with our expectations. We want an abundant life and we may experience cancer or another debilitating illness. We want a happy family life and we may experience rebellious children or marital difficulties. We want a fulfilling career and we experience a bad boss or no chance of promotion. Our lives can be full of "Egypts." Even the Lord Jesus had to go to Egypt as a baby with Mary and Joseph; God's trail may have many switchbacks and detours.

Abram had to go to Egypt, but God had promised to keep him safe: *"I will bless those who bless you, and whoever curses you I will curse."* (Genesis 12:3) But he was only human, and decided to help God out a little. He developed a "plan B" with Sarai, his wife.

> *As he was about to enter Egypt, he said to his wife Sarai, "I know what a beautiful woman you are. When the Egyptians see you, they will say, 'This is his wife.' Then they will kill me but will let you live. Say you are my sister, so I will be treated well for your sake and my life will be spared because of you." (Genesis 12:11-13)*

Abram thought he had everything figured out. He had concluded that when the Egyptians saw Sarai and found out she was his wife, they would certainly kill him. He told his wife Sarai to tell everyone that she was his sister, not his wife. This way he reasoned his life would be spared. He decided to hedge his bets a little just for added insurance. In other words, he lied and put his wife's chastity in jeopardy to save his own skin. To make matters worse, he even thought he could become richer by this deception.

Why would Abram do this? Well, remember, he did not know God that well yet. He did not have the book of Proverbs to open and read: *"Trust in the LORD with all your heart and lean not on your own understanding."* (Proverbs 3:5) We probably would have been tempted to act just as he did. And what a mess he was making!

Abram's ruse turned out to be a problematic decision. Sure enough, Pharaoh noticed Sarai and took her into his house to be a part of his harem. Now what was Abram supposed to do? He was in a real pickle. Imagine his sense of desperation and perhaps even guilt. How was Sarai going to bear him the son God had promised when she was in the harem of Pharaoh? His actions had caused consequences for other people, too – especially Sarai and Pharoah. He had painted himself and others into a corner.

But God graciously rescued Abram and Sarai. He inflicted disease on the royal house and Pharaoh quickly figured out the root of the problem. Pharaoh summoned Abram, and rebuked him for lying, but did not punish him. By this time, Pharaoh was probably frightened of the power behind this man. (Genesis 12:17-20) By a miraculous rescue, Abram, Sarai and their household were delivered from Egypt, and left even wealthier than when they entered the country.

The entire Egyptian affair looked like a geographical mistake on God's part. It was so "beside the point" on the surface. But God had his reasons, even though Abram may have never learned what they were. God was good at His word and would protect him regardless of his circumstances. Perhaps in the future Abram would not try to help God out again. Or maybe he was a slow learner like us.

Family Squabbles and Dangers

Abram's life became even more complicated, as we read in chapters 13 and 14 of Genesis. He and Lot had both become very wealthy, and their herdsmen began to quarrel over land and water rights. It was time for them to part company. Abram made an incredibly generous offer as patriarch, and this showed the kind of a man he was: he let Lot choose the land he wanted, and he was willing to take the leftovers. Lot chose the whole plain of the Jordan and settled near the cities of the plain. He pitched his tents near Sodom. (Genesis 13:12)

After Lot's departure, the Lord restated his promise to Abram:

> *"Lift up your eyes from where you are and look north and south, east and west. All the land that you see I will give to you and your offspring forever. I will make your offspring like the dust of the earth, so that if anyone could count the dust, then your offspring could be counted. Go, walk through the length and breadth of the land, for I am giving it to you." (Genesis 13:14-17)*

There it was again – the dual promise of land and an heir. They were linked together in Abram's mind. Maybe this restatement by God meant that their fulfillment was at hand? If I were Abram, the cynic in me would have something to say to God when he started talking about not being able to count descendants. I might say, *"I can count my* descendants right now, Lord, and the number is zero!" Yet in response, Abram built another altar to God in Hebron.

God did not seem to be in any hurry to fulfill his promises to Abram. What happened next seems like another detour or wrong turn. You can read all the details is Genesis 14.

Lot was in trouble, and this impacted Abram. Lot had been captured and taken away as a result of getting caught up in a local war. Abram felt compelled to muster his 318 men and rescue his nephew, which he did. Mobilizing his resources and fighting several tribal kings was risky business, yet Abram forged ahead for the sake of his extended family. After he was successful (it had to have been a close call), Abram had the opportunity to become even wealthier by keeping the spoils of war, but he refused to do so. He was blessed by the mysterious priest Melchizedek, and the family crisis seemed to have passed. At least one of them.

Getting Questions Answered

After this rescue, God appeared to Abram again and restated his threefold promise of protection, an heir, and possession of the land of Canaan. But this time in Genesis Chapter 15, Abram spilled the beans. He spoke up to God and brought up the issue of not having a child to inherit anything. It was, after all, "the elephant in the room."

"O Sovereign LORD, what can you give me since I remain childless...?" (Genesis 15:2)

God then clarified his promise that his own biological child would become his heir. This seemed to settle the matter (at least temporarily) for Abram, for we read in verse 6: *"Abram believed the LORD, and he credited to him as righteousness."*

This is one of the most remarkable and theologically packed statements in all of Scripture. The Apostle Paul refers to this passage when making his argument for justification by faith in Romans. But for our purposes, suffice it to say that Abram had absolute faith in God's promises. But he addressed the issue of possessing the land in verse 8: *"O Sovereign LORD, how can I know that I will gain possession of it?"*

God then entered a covenant of blood with Abram and then went on to tell him a little of what his descendants would have to suffer before the land of Canaan truly became their own.

There is a powerful Biblical principle illustrated in this passage. It seems OK for a person in a relationship with God to ask questions and express doubts. Abram asked, "How can this be?" and "How can I know?" Abram was growing in his relationship with God – enough to the point where he felt secure enough to ask God questions. God accepted these questions and even gave answers to Abram. It seems that God reveals His answers piecemeal in His own good time. Fortunately for Abram, he received some answers to his questions that sustained him for his journey of faith. But he only received these answers because he asked the questions! We too are invited to ask God our tough questions. We may not get all the answers we want, but if we are patient, we will get the answers we need.

Through subsequent encounters with God, Abram was given a new name – Abraham – the father of many nations. (Genesis 17:5) Sarai was renamed Sarah – princess and mother of nations and kings. (Genesis 17:15-16) New names in this ancient culture implied a new identity and direction in life. This certainly was the case with Abraham and Sarah.

The Complication of Hager and Ishmael

Although they had received new names, there were still a lot of old habits and fears to break. Abraham and Sarah were old. Sarah was past child bearing years. She devised a solution that was logical to any human mind in this culture.

> *"The LORD has kept me from having children. Go, sleep with my maidservant; perhaps I can build a family through her." (Genesis 16:2)*

Abraham was asked to conceive a child-heir with Hagar, Sarah's servant girl. On the surface, this was a perfect way to help God along to fulfill His promise. *"Why not help God create a 'straight path' in our lives?"* they might be asking. It was another "plan B" moment for Abraham and Sarah. But it was the spiritual equivalent to a football halfback running in front of his blockers – ultimately not a good idea. It would have been better to wait for things to develop as intended according to the rules of the game.

The result was that Hagar did have a son – Ishmael. And Abraham loved this boy. But this "straight path solution" ultimately created strife in the family – especially between Sarah and Hagar. It was a complication and ultimately not God's solution. This step was Sarah's and Abraham's doing – *"let's help God out in fulfilling his promises."* Amazingly, God did not write them off or negate His plan, but instead bestowed grace to everyone concerned. God promised to bless Hagar and Ishmael. (Genesis 16:11-12; 21:17)

Isaac – Finally!

Abraham and Sarah were not getting any younger. In Genesis 18, God sent three visitors. They were on their way to judge Sodom, but they also made a specific promise to the couple. *"I will surely return to you about this time next year, and Sarah your wife will have a son."* (Genesis 18:10)

Sarah laughed at this news, and thereby named her future child Isaac, which meant "laughter." Notice that God finally gave Abraham and Sarah a firm timeline for Isaac's birth. How long they had waited for this information! After waiting a lifetime, now they only had to wait one more year. And God's covenant would be fulfilled through Isaac, the child of the promise. (Genesis 21:12b)

The elderly couple had only one year left to see God's long-awaited promise fulfilled. And yet, we read in Genesis 20 that Abram was still open to some "plan B" thinking. He was living as a foreigner in the region of the Philistines, and he repeated his Egyptian mistake – this time with a local king named Abimelek.

> *Now Abraham moved on from there into the region of the Negev and lived between Kadesh and Shur. For a while he stayed in Gerar, and there Abraham said of his wife Sarah, "She is my sister." Then Abimelek king of Gerar sent for Sarah and took her. (Genesis 20:1-2)*

God intervened again, and warned the pagan king that Sarah was Abraham's wife, and the situation was once again resolved. But Abraham made the same mistake twice, showing he was only human. He tended to give in to fear when threatened and developed his own backup plan. He tried to rely on human insurance. This was a pattern in Abraham's walk with God. He brought Lot with him when God told him to leave his family – might this have been a form of human insurance? Later, he lied to Pharoah about Sarah. He tried to have the promised heir through a slave woman Hagar. And he lied again to Abimelek, knowing God's promised child was less than a year away. I find it comforting that this "friend of God" was far from a perfect man. He had times of worry and fear, just like me. God was patient and faithful to His promise and plan, and continued to walk with Abraham to make him the man He wanted him to be.

I have heard it said: "God is always on time, but He is seldom early." That certainly was the case for Abraham and Sarah. In the fullness of time – 24 years after he first called Abraham – God gave them a son. There was great rejoicing and laughter. What Abraham and Sarah had waited for took most of their lifetimes, but at the moment of Isaac's birth, it all seemed worthwhile.

Sacrifice My Son?

There are few "happily ever after moments" in Abraham's life story. We might expect after Isaac was born, God would bless him and let Abraham live in peace and die without any more struggles or tests.

But God was not finished yet.

God asked Abraham to do something that sounded completely out of character with His divine nature. He asked Abraham to sacrifice his son on an altar as an act of worship to God. This was in line with how ancient pagans worshipped, but it was a tremendous test for Abraham. It begs the question: why would God give Abraham a son and then ask him to kill him? How could God's promise of an heir from his union with Sarah possibly be fulfilled if Abraham obeyed God?

Of all the zigs and zags in Abraham's life, this was the biggest. I must confess, if I were Abraham, this may have pushed me over the edge. But Abraham must have remembered how faithful God had been to him over all the years of his life. We read in Hebrews 11:19 that *"Abraham reasoned that God could even raise the dead, and so in a manner of speaking he did receive Isaac back from death."*

So, Abraham believed and obeyed. And this time – finally – *he devised no "plan B."* If this was Abraham's final exam in the school of faith, he passed with an A+. God saw that Abraham would not withhold anything from his Lord – even his only son. God provided a substitute sacrifice and restated his promise to bless Abraham richly. (Genesis 22:16-18)

The Genesis narrative then lays out a few more tasks for Abraham – including burying his beloved wife Sarah and finding a wife for his son. God's redemptive story passed on to Isaac and his descendants. This brings us to the end of Abraham's story. He died at the age of 175.

The End of the Line

Abraham finished well. What can we learn from looking at this remarkable life?

- God moved through "switchbacks" according to his own timetable and purpose. God caused many of the zigs and zags in Abraham's life: the famine that led him to Egypt; wars making it necessary for him to rescue Lot; and a lifetime of infertility. Learning from Abraham's life can become a cure for our own hurried, dissatisfied lives – to see this man's growing patience and how all these experiences led him to know God better. At the end, Abraham was called a "friend of God." (James 2:23)

- Some of the zigs and zags in Abraham's life were a result of his own sin, doubts and struggles: perhaps bringing Lot along was one of these; others definitely included deceiving Pharaoh and later Abimelek; and having a child with Hagar. All these were a result of "plan B" thinking and seeking to provide human insurance and security in his life. Through it all, God showed love and grace to Abraham and his family. God worked his plan out even through Abraham's mistakes. We must remember that Abraham had no Bible to study. He learned bit by bit about God throughout his lifetime. God also wants us to trust Him completely and let go of our "plan B" thinking.

- Traveling the crooked path in life according to God's plan made Abraham's act of faith possible. He ultimately discarded his "plan B" thinking, and was willing to sacrifice his son, Isaac. God had proven himself faithful, and so Abraham could trust and obey.

Why did God wait until Abraham and Sarah were very old to give them their son? We may not know the complete reason, but we see God received the glory because of it. In the end, God was good at his word. He did make Abraham a great nation. He did give the people of Israel the Promised Land. And he did bless the entire world through this one man by bringing Jesus, as Lord and Christ, through his line. God would sacrifice His only Son for the salvation of the world.

The opportunity for God to provide straight paths for Abraham to walk in was always there. But God in His wisdom had his reasons why he made very few of them. And look at the person that emerged.

Questions for Reflection and Discussion

1. How difficult do you think it was for Abram and his household to obey God and leave familiar surroundings? Have you ever had to make such a life-changing decision? How did you respond?

2. To survive the famine, Abram had to move his household again. How would you have reacted to the famine in the land of Canaan? This was unexpected for him – especially in light of what God had promised to do for him. Have you had similar

tests of your faith? What did God do in your circumstances, and what did you do?

3. What evidence is there in Abraham's story that he was a fallible human being – just like us? How did God work through Abraham's "plan B" thinking to work out His divine plan?

4. Trace the events of Abraham's journey of faith. How can you see God teaching him to trust him more and more as his life unfolded? Why do you think Abraham finally came to the point of being willing to sacrifice his only son to the LORD? (Hebrews 11:17-19 might give you some kind of an answer).

David Rox

Switchbacks

2

The Rugged Road: JACOB

My years have been few and difficult. (Genesis 47:9)

In order to learn why Jacob said this at the end of his life, we will take a look at his story beginning in Genesis 25. From his very birth, Jacob's life seemed to be a continual struggle.

Background

Jacob was the grandson of Abraham and Sarah. Like Sarah, Abraham's daughter-in-law Rebekah took a long time to get pregnant. But when she finally did, she was pregnant with twins. Two babies were wrestling in her womb. Rebekah asked the Lord what was going on, and He told her:

> *"Two nations are in your womb, and two peoples from within you will be separated; one people will be stronger than the other, and the older will serve the younger." (Genesis 25:23)*

Rebekah had twin sons, and she named them Esau and Jacob. It was clear from the start that they were not identical twins. Esau was a rugged redhead, and Jacob was a grabber. He came out of the womb grabbing Esau's heel, and this foreshadowed their life stories as siblings.

The term "dysfunctional family" seems almost redundant. All families are to some extent, and the family of Isaac, Rebekah, Esau and Jacob was no exception. The father Isaac favored Esau, because he was an outdoorsman. Rebekah favored her second son. Jacob was to become a bit of a "mama's boy."

While they are still quite young, we read of an episode where Esau came in from the outdoors famished to the point of insanity. Jacob was cooking a red stew and Esau asks for some. Jacob, being a grabber from birth, saw this as an opportunity to bargain for his brother's birthright. Esau thought about his stomach, while Jacob thought about acquiring more possessions. Esau sold his rights as a firstborn son for a bowl of stew. It seemed Esau was not into delayed gratification. We are told that by this simple act he despised his birthright. (Genesis 25:34) Jacob knew where to hit his brother where he was the weakest – his stomach. So, Jacob first grabbed the heel of Esau and then his birthright. But Jacob was not finished with his grabbing.

Robbery and Flight

As Isaac grew old and feeble, he chose a time to bestow his blessing upon Esau – to make him the one through whom God's covenant would pass. This was a big deal. Oral pronouncements and end-of-life bequests were legal and binding in this culture. With his mother's help, Jacob grabbed the blessing – or stole it, to be more precise. Rebekah and Jacob used deception, disguise, and food to dupe poor Isaac. He bestowed his richest blessing upon the younger son Jacob, and Esau had to settle for the leftovers. It was a legal swindle and it was irrevocable.

Rebekah and Jacob were schemers and co-conspirators. As we shall see, it seemed swindling ran in Rebekah's family. Wait till you meet Laban, Jacob's uncle!

Understandably, Esau held a strong grudge and planned to murder Jacob once his father Isaac was dead. Rebekah, ever vigilant, got wind of it. Really, how hard could that be? The anger of redheads can be legendary. She planned to send Jacob away to Haran – where Abraham lived prior to God's calling him. Both parents wanted Jacob to get a wife from Laban's household rather than a pagan wife from Canaan.

Let's pause to reflect a moment. Some questions pop into my mind. Is this really God's chosen line? Are these the kind of people God would use to work out His perfect plan? How could God work through such a dysfunctional family? But then again, what other kind of family is there for God to work through?

Isaac sent Jacob away with a blessing, making it clear he knew the promise to Abraham had been passed down to Jacob and not Esau.

> *"May God Almighty bless you and make you fruitful and increase your numbers until you become a community of peoples. May he give you and your descendants the blessing given to Abraham, so that you may take possession of the land where you now reside as a foreigner, the land God gave to Abraham." (Genesis 28:3-4)*

Bethel

So, Jacob fled from his brother to Haran. He was on the run and had nothing with him except his walking stick. On his journey, Jacob had a dream at Luz (or, as he named the place, Bethel). The Lord appeared to him, perhaps for the first time in his life, and reiterated the covenantal promises to Abraham.

> *"I am the LORD, the God of your father Abraham and the God of Isaac. I will give you and your descendants the land on which you are lying. Your descendants will be like the dust of the earth, and you will spread out to the west and to the east, to the north and to the south. All peoples on earth will be blessed through you and your offspring. I am with you and will watch over you wherever you go, and I will bring you back to this land. I will not leave you until I have done what I have promised you." (Genesis 28:13-15)*

God graciously promised to bless and work in the life of this young swindler. This was good news to Jacob, as he was alone and penniless. God was promising to protect him and guard his future. This made quite an impression on the young man.

> *Then Jacob made a vow, saying, "If God will be with me and will watch over me on this journey I am taking and will give me food to eat and clothes to wear so that I return safely to my father's household, then the LORD will be my God and this stone that I have set up as a pillar will be God's house, and of all that you give me I will give you a tenth." (Genesis 28:20-22)*

Jacob indulged in a little conditional bargaining with God. *"If God takes care of me, then I will worship Him."* Perhaps he moved on to Haran with renewed confidence and optimism. Perhaps he was expecting an easy time of it in the land of his relatives. However, there was no simple straight path about to appear. Rather, several twists and turns awaited Jacob.

Twenty Years of Hard Labor

If Jacob thought God would bless him quickly and easily, he was sadly mistaken. The next years were not going to be easy ones. What lay ahead for Jacob was 20 years of hard labor, and being enrolled in God's "school of faith."

Jacob traveled to Haran and met Rachel, a distant cousin. It was a classic case of love at first sight. He eventually met his mother Rebekah's brother, Laban, who welcomed Jacob into his household. Jacob became a paid employee, and the two men negotiated wages. Jacob wanted Rachel as his bride, and Laban agreed in return for seven years of work. To me, this deal seems a little lopsided in favor of Laban. The uncle was getting the better part of the bargain. But Jacob was so in love with Rachel that the seven years flew by.

What happened after the seven-year period was remarkable. Jacob, the grabber, got swindled himself in a big way. Laban pulled a fast one on the unsuspecting Jacob, and brought his older, less comely daughter Leah to his bed on the wedding night. In the days before electricity, Jacob did not discover this until the morning light. *"When morning came, there was Leah!"* (Genesis 29:25) The swindler was out-swindled. And like the situation with stealing Esau's blessing, it was a legal swindle and it was irrevocable.

Laban explained it was the custom in the land not to marry off a younger daughter before her older sister. For another seven years of labor, Jacob could have Rachel as well. Uncle Laban's deal for Jacob was two sisters and their two servant girls, all in one package, in return for a total of 14 years of work as a shepherd.

While Abraham and Isaac had trouble having children, Jacob did not. Not only does this period of Jacob's life involve hard labor for him, it also involved hard labor for his four wives, Leah. Rachel, and the servant girls Zilpah and Bilhah.

Marriage is difficult between one man and one woman. It is far more complicated when it involves multiple wives. In Genesis 29 and 30, we read of some competitive birthing in Jacob's new family. Familial favoritism reared its head in this generation as it had in the past. Leah was not loved as much as Rachel. Leah had babies, but Rachel had none. Rachel did what Sarah did two generations earlier – she gave her servant girl Bilhah to her husband to have children for her. Leah responded by giving her servant girl Zilpah. The baby competition was off and running.

Names given to children were very important in this culture. The names given to the sons of Jacob by their mothers showed that unhealthy wrangling was underway. Just look at the running account of the baby competition.

- Reuben (Leah) – "Look! A Son!"

- Simeon (Leah) – "Because the Lord heard that I am not loved."

- Levi (Leah) – "Now my husband will be attached to me."

- Judah (Leah) – "This time I will praise the Lord."

- Dan (Rachel via Bilhah) – "God has vindicated me for my childlessness."

- Naphtali (Rachel via Bilhah) – "I have had a great struggle with my sister, and I have won."
- Gad (Leah via Zilpah) – "What good luck!"
- Asher (Leah via Zilpah) – "How happy I am!"
- Issacher (Leah) – "God has rewarded me for giving my maidservant to my husband."
- Zebulun (Leah) – "This time my husband will treat me with honor, for I have borne him 6 sons."
- Joseph (Rachel) – "God has taken away my disgrace – may he give me another son."

Imagine the family dynamics with four competing wives and all those children milling around in one place!

As for Laban during these years, the Lord had blessed him because of Jacob, and he did not want to part with him. Both Jacob and Laban realized God's hand had been at work. After fourteen years of service to Laban, Jacob signed up for another six years to gain flocks and possessions of his own.

Jacob made a modest request of Laban. Sheep were generally all white, and goats all black. Jacob was willing to take only streaked or spotted animals for his pay, and leave the normal ones for Laban and his sons. Laban agreed, but secretly and without Jacob's knowledge, he removed all the existing streaked or spotted animals from the herds Jacob was tending. On the surface, it is a story of two connivers trying to outdo each other. Laban tried to stack the deck against Jacob to increase his wealth at Jacob's expense, but God caused Jacob's flocks to increase in spite of Laban's schemes. Long-time Gordon College Professor of Biblical Studies, Dr. Marvin Wilson, rightly refers to these antics as "the survival of the slickest."

Time to Move On

In Genesis 31, we read that Laban's attitude started to sour towards Jacob. His own sons were bitter and envious of Jacob's prosperity. They believed it was coming at their expense. It was time for Jacob to leave before things got ugly.

Jacob was told by God to leave. He complained to his wives:

> *"You know that I've worked for your father with all my strength, yet your father has cheated me by changing my wages ten times. However, God has not allowed him to harm me." (Genesis 31:6-7)*

Jacob then fled without telling Laban he was going. To make matters more tense, Rachel stole Laban's household gods before leaving. This is more evidence that underhandedness and theft ran in the family. Upon learning of the flight and the theft, Laban pursued Jacob and his daughters with violence on his mind. But God warned Laban in a dream not to harm Jacob. When Laban and his men caught up with Jacob at Mizpah, it was a tension-filled situation. Laban accused Jacob of theft and leaving without saying goodbye. Even though Rachel did steal the household gods, they were not found due to Rachel's deception.

Laban rebuked Jacob for leaving:

> *"What have you done? You've deceived me, and you've carried off my daughters like captives in war. Why did you run off secretly and deceive me? Why didn't you tell me, so I could send you away with joy and singing to the music of timbrels and harps? You didn't even let me kiss my grandchildren and my daughters goodbye. You have done a foolish thing. I have the power to harm you; but last night the God of your father said to me, 'Be careful not to say anything to Jacob, either good or bad.'" (Genesis 31;26-29)*

Jacob took this occasion to make his true feelings known to Laban:

> *"I have been with you for twenty years now. Your sheep and goats have not miscarried, nor have I eaten rams from your flocks. I did not bring you animals torn by wild beasts; I bore the loss myself. And you demanded payment from me for whatever was stolen by day or night. This was my situation: The heat consumed me in the daytime and the cold at night, and sleep fled from my eyes. It was like this for the twenty years I was in your household. I worked for you fourteen years for your two daughters and six years for your flocks, and you changed my wages ten times. If the God of my father, the God of Abraham and the Fear of Isaac, had not been with me, you would surely have sent me away empty-handed. But God has seen my hardship and the toil of my hands, and last night he rebuked you." (Genesis 31:38-42)*

After this confrontation, Jacob departed from Laban after making a peace treaty. The words of the "Mizpah benediction" were pronounced: *"May the LORD keep watch between you and me when we are away from each other."* (Genesis 31:49) It was less than an amicable parting between these men.

Jacob was now moving out of one dangerous situation into another one. It was time to meet Esau again.

Facing the Music

Jacob had been told by God to return to his family. This meant returning to the brother he had cheated. Jacob decided to send messengers to his brother ahead of time saying he was returning. He was handling Esau with kid gloves, for he knew he might still be angry enough to kill him after 20 years. When his messengers returned, they told Jacob his brother was coming to meet him with 400 men. Not good news!

Jacob suspected the worst and prepared to save what he could of his family and possessions. He divided his entourage into two groups, so if Esau attacked one group, the other might escape.

This crisis brought Jacob to the point of prayer. He cried out to God for safety and rescue. For the first time in his story, we see Jacob humbling himself before God. We read the desperate prayer of a grabber – one who has striven his whole life in his own strength.

> *Then Jacob prayed, "O God of my father Abraham, God of my father Isaac, LORD, you who said to me, 'Go back to your country and your relatives, and I will make you prosper,' I am unworthy of all the kindness and faithfulness you have shown your servant. I had only my staff when I crossed this Jordan, but now I have become two camps. Save me, I pray, from the hand of my brother Esau, for I am afraid he will come and attack me, and also the mothers with their children. But you have said, 'I will surely make you prosper and will make your descendants like the sand of the sea, which cannot be counted.'" (Gen. 32:9-12)*

Jacob decided to approach Esau humbly and sent gifts ahead of himself – extravagant gifts of livestock designed to arrive in a number of waves. He instructed his servants to address Esau as "lord" and to describe Jacob to Esau as "your servant." Jacob was doing all he could to placate his brother and to diffuse his anger.

Alone and Wrestling

This was the great crisis moment in Jacob's life. All his deception and grabbing were coming home to roost in this meeting with his brother. Before the fateful meeting, Jacob spent the night all alone. His night was a sleepless one. We read in Genesis 32:24 that a mysterious man – or more likely an angel – appeared and wrestled with Jacob until daybreak.

It was quite a match. The stranger could not overpower Jacob, and Jacob would not let him go. After all, he was "the grabber." Through this experience, Jacob got a dislocated hip socket and a new name: Israel – one who strives with God. It appears that a spiritual transaction had taken place, and Jacob was changed.

If Jacob was going to have to fight with Esau now, he would be limping and virtually incapacitated. He was a physical invalid. This was part of God's plan – Jacob's strength from God would have to be perfected in weakness. He was utterly dependent upon God and his provision.

But surprisingly, Jacob was met with love and favor by Esau. It appeared that time had softened his heart and healed old wounds. Esau too had prospered over the past 20 years and seemed to hold no hard feelings against his younger brother.

The Later Years

In spite of the grace-filled reception Jacob received from Esau, Jacob's life after his return to Canaan was far from trouble-free. He settled in Shechem in Canaan. His daughter Dinah was subsequently raped by the Shechemites, and his sons wreaked vengeance upon them by murdering the entire clan. The Lord then directed him to move to Bethel, where God had appeared to him when he was fleeing from his brother twenty years earlier. There he settled down for a time and built an altar to the Lord. After moving on from Bethel, his favorite wife Rachel became pregnant again, but died in childbirth. Jacob's last son was Benjamin, whose name means "son of my right hand." As we shall see, his two sons with Rachel, Joseph and Benjamin, became his favorites.

Jacob was able to return to Canaan in time to be there when his father Isaac died. After this, the Genesis account involving Jacob, or Israel as he was later named, became caught up in the story of Joseph. This is examined in the next chapter.

Suffice it to say that Jacob's later years were far from peaceful. They were full of grief over the loss of his beloved wife, the perceived loss of his favorite son Joseph, the heartaches of dealing with lying and unruly sons (his oldest son Reuben slept with one of his concubines), the difficult task of overseeing great possessions in a nomadic culture, and the pains of enduring famine and uncertainty.

It is interesting to note when Jacob met Pharaoh toward the end of his life, he was asked by Pharaoh about his age and experience. In Genesis 47:9, we read his response: *"The years of my pilgrimage are a hundred and thirty. My years have been few and difficult. And they do not equal the years of the pilgrimage of my fathers."*

Final Blessings

The final scenes involving Jacob are given in Genesis 48 and 49. In the last days of his life – now living in Egypt – Jacob spoke to his long-lost son Joseph of things that were most important to him.

> *Jacob said to Joseph, "God Almighty appeared to me at Luz in the land of Canaan, and there he blessed me and said to me, 'I am going to make you fruitful and increase your numbers. I will make you a community of peoples, and I will give this land as an everlasting possession to your descendants after you.'*
>
> *"Now then, your two sons born to you in Egypt before I came to you here will be reckoned as mine; Ephraim and Manasseh will be mine, just as Reuben and Simeon are mine. Any children born to you after them will be yours; in the territory they inherit they will be reckoned under the names of their brothers. As I was returning from Paddan, to my sorrow Rachel died in the land of Canaan while we were still on the way, a little distance from Ephrath. So I buried her there beside the road to Ephrath" (that is, Bethlehem). (Genesis 48:3-7)*

Jacob hearkened back to two events in his life: his experience at Luz (Bethel), where the Lord first appeared to him. He remembered God's initial promise to protect him and bless him, and to fulfill God's covenant to Abraham's children. Secondly, he grieved over the loss of Rachel, Joseph's mother. He bestowed a special honor on Joseph by treating Manasseh and Ephraim as his own sons, giving them equal inheritance. But he added a twist to this blessing: the younger son Ephraim would be greater than the older son Manasseh, much to the chagrin of Joseph.

> *Then he blessed Joseph and said, "May the God before whom my fathers Abraham and Isaac walked faithfully, the God who has been my shepherd all my life to this day, the Angel who has delivered me from all harm – may he bless*

these boys. May they be called by my name and the names of my fathers Abraham and Isaac, and may they increase greatly on the earth."

When Joseph saw his father placing his right hand on Ephraim's head he was displeased; so he took hold of his father's hand to move it from Ephraim's head to Manasseh's head. Joseph said to him, "No, my father, this one is the firstborn; put your right hand on his head." But his father refused and said, "I know, my son, I know. He too will become a people, and he too will become great. Nevertheless, his younger brother will be greater than he, and his descendants will become a group of nations." He blessed them that day and said, "In your name will Israel pronounce this blessing: 'May God make you like Ephraim and Manasseh.'" So he put Ephraim ahead of Manasseh. (Genesis 48:15-20)

So, generations before David wrote Psalm 23 where Israel's king called the Lord his shepherd, Jacob used the same image. I find it interesting that this life-long shepherd, at the end of his life, referred to God as *his shepherd,* and he recognized that the Lord's angels protected him every step along his way. After this pronouncement, he declared that the younger brother would be greater than the older brother, mirroring his own experience.

The patriarch Israel then gathered all his sons together and pronounced blessings upon them all before dying a peaceful death.

The End of the Line

What can we learn from the story of Jacob?

- God can even use a sly, selfish, ambitious person from a dysfunctional family – a "grabber" – for his purposes and glory. And He chooses whomever he wants. He does not always choose the oldest and the strongest; He can work in spite of the dysfunctional relationships in a family to work out his purposes. God doesn't completely reject mothers or sons just because they play favorites, practice deception and greed, or are imperfect in a myriad of ways. After all, what other kind of human beings can God find? That is grace!

- As we see time and time again, God's plan unfolds over long stretches of time – in Jacob's case, over 20 years of hard labor under a bad boss. When God appeared to Jacob at Bethel at the beginning of his story, Jacob did not know what trials lay ahead of him. Yet, through it all, God was faithful and good at His word.

Switchbacks

- God revealed himself to Jacob in a time of great crisis and struggle. Before he met Esau, Jacob had to meet God anew, and he had to wrestle with Him all night. Imagine how exhausting this must have been! And yet, when the morning came, he was transformed and given a new name and identity. God often transforms us through crisis and struggle as well. It is a central part of the human experience.

- Jacob's life reminds us that life leaves scars. Jacob limped until his dying day after his all-night wrestling match with God, and he grieved the death of his beloved Rachel till the end of his life. Certainly, his years of grieving over the perceived loss of Joseph took a great toll as well. But in the midst of these woes, his life still had meaning and goodness. Our lives are no different. God proves himself faithful in the long run.

- In the end, Jacob looked at God as his faithful, lifelong shepherd, his guard and protector. Through all his fears and toil, Jacob came to know that his God stood with him. His life was not an easy one; our lives often prove no different.

Jacob was transformed from "the grabber" to "Israel" – the one who strives with God. His favorite son would be known not as a grabber, but a dreamer. We turn next to Joseph and his amazing story.

Questions for Reflection and Discussion

1. What is your reaction to the dysfunctionality in Jacob's family? When have you had to deal with cheating, lying, favoritism, deception and anger depicted early on in this story?

2. If you met Jacob, do you think you would have liked him? What in his personality might make it difficult being his friend?

3. Laban was not a good boss. Have you had tough working conditions similar to Jacob's?

4. Describe the family dynamics brought about by Jacob having four wives who were all mothers of his children.

5. What do you think is the major turning point in Jacob's life? How did God strengthen Jacob's faith and lead him to the point where he was willing to declare that the LORD was "his shepherd?" (Genesis 48:15)

David Rox

Switchbacks

3

Traversing Highs and Lows: JOSEPH

"You intended to harm me, but God intended it for good...." (Genesis 50:20a)

Perhaps Joseph would win the prize for walking the most zig-zag life's trail in the Bible. His story dominates the latter chapters of Genesis. It is significant that the book of Genesis ends with the story of Joseph. Why Joseph? Why is he so important? We learn when we read his entire life's story that he was God's instrument of deliverance – the means for God to work out His plan and process. The book of Genesis ends with the people of Israel in Egypt.

Background

By the time we get to Genesis 37, we have been introduced to Jacob's very large family – twelve sons! The first thing we read about Joseph (son number 11) as a 17-year-old is that he was a tattle tale. He was out tending his father's flocks with several of his half-brothers, and *"he brought their father a bad report about them."* (Gen. 37:2) We are not told the nature of the bad report, but it was probably true back then as it is now: no one likes a stool pigeon. Joseph could not have been the most popular sibling with his brothers after this incident.

Then we read a little about the dysfunctionality in Jacob's household. He loved Joseph more than his other sons, because he was the firstborn of his favorite wife Rachel, who by this time in the story had died. Joseph was the apple of his father's eye, born to him in his old age.

Jacob honored Joseph by making a long-flowing robe for him. Although it probably wasn't "the amazing technicolor dream coat," Joseph's father meant this to honor Joseph, and so it did. But it also had some other effects.

> *"When his brothers saw that their father loved [Joseph] more than any of them, they hated him and could not speak a kind word to him." (Gen. 37:4)*

Sadly, favoritism in families is common. In Joseph's case it was to prove downright dangerous.

The Dreamer

If Jacob could be nicknamed "the grabber," Joseph could be nicknamed "the dreamer." If receiving his father's present of a fancy coat weren't bad enough to anger his brothers, Joseph then had two dreams. Dreams were significant in the ancient world, and Joseph naively shared his dreams with his family. *"Listen to this dream I had,"* he said innocently. (Genesis 37:6) He then related how they were binding sheaves of grain at harvest time. His sheaf stood tall while all the others bowed down before it. The brothers were quick to understand the interpretation – Joseph was saying he would become superior to them and reign over them. So, they hated him all the more.

Then Joseph had a second dream, and he once again shared it with his family. This time the sun and moon and eleven stars all bowed down to him. When hearing the second dream, Jacob himself rebuked his son:

> *"What is this dream you had? Will your mother and I and your brothers actually come and bow down to the ground before you?" (Genesis 37:10)*

It seems the entire family was able to interpret Joseph's dreams. If we put ourselves into this family situation, not yet knowing how the story will ultimately end, we would probably have a similar reaction to this teenage boy. He was his father's favorite and it had gone to his head. He was an over-confident, conceited tattle tale and a fairly obnoxious young man with a superiority complex. Hatred was brewing and was leading to a family explosion.

The fancy coat, his father's playing favorites, and his sharing his dreams all proved hazardous to Joseph's health.

Trouble in Dothan

Beginning in Genesis 37:12, we see the unfolding of the first major zig-zag in Joseph's life. It started innocently enough. Jacob sent Joseph on a fact-finding mission to his brothers and the flocks in Shechem. Jacob wanted to know if all was well. He sent Joseph, who he knew was a fair and balanced reporter. If there was anything wrong, Joseph would be sure to let his father know.

Joseph departed and finally tracked down his brothers and the flocks at Dothan. His brothers saw him coming from quite a way off – the coat probably gave Joseph away. The sight of Joseph didn't exactly fill his brothers with familial affection. All their bitterness came to the fore:

> "Here comes that dreamer!" they said to each other. "Come now, let's kill him and throw him into one of these cisterns and say that a ferocious animal devoured him. Then we'll see what comes of his dreams." (Gen. 37:19-20)

Now we see just how bad these family dynamics had gotten!

The eldest brother Reuben negotiated with his brothers to spare Joseph's life. He alone wanted to restore Joseph to his father. He succeeded in staying Joseph's execution, but circumstances took a turn that moved Joseph away from complete rescue and restoration to his father.

When Joseph arrived to his brothers' camp, they stripped him of his robe and threw him into an empty cistern. Then they left him there and sat down to eat. Meanwhile, undoubtedly Joseph was frantically pleading for his life, and begging his brothers for mercy. But to no avail. Some Ishmaelite merchants travelled by on their way to Egypt, and Judah, one of the brothers, hit upon a new and improved idea:

> "What will we gain if we kill our brother and cover up his blood? Come, let's sell him to the Ishmaelites and not lay our hands on him; after all, he is our brother, our own flesh and blood." (Gen. 37:26-27)

What virtue Judah showed here! They sold the wailing Joseph to the travelers for twenty shekels of silver. Joseph was off to Egypt as a slave, without his special coat.

This would be a major turn-around in anyone's life – going from favorite son to a pit in the wilderness to traveling to a foreign land as a slave. And betrayed by one's own brothers! Life could be over at the age of seventeen. If ever a person had the right to grow bitter and angry, it was Joseph.

To say Joseph was wronged by his brothers is a gross understatement. And the father Jacob was also wronged. The brothers had to construct a lie they would live with for many years to come: Supposedly, Joseph was killed by a wild animal. In this family, it becomes the family secret for a long time. The brothers lied to their father and then watched him painfully grieve his life away.

The Good Life in Egypt – for a While

Joseph was taking an unexpected trip to Egypt, just like his great-grandfather Abraham had done. But Joseph was going as a slave, not a visitor. If he struggled with any thoughts of being a victim, he did not let them destroy him. In Genesis 39, we read that he was sold as a slave to Potiphar, one of Pharaoh's officials, the captain of the guard. We read the Lord was with Joseph, and he prospered. (Gen. 39:2) Here Joseph showed his worth as a slave. He became so valued by Potiphar for his efficiency that he was put in charge of the entire household. He was trusted with everything by Potiphar, and made a personal attendant within the official's affairs. So, it seemed like Joseph's new life was not going to turn out so bad after all. He was a favorite in a new family. Potiphar almost became like a second father to Joseph. This young man seemed to be able to "bloom where he was planted."

Joseph demonstrated a good head for business even as a young man, and became practically indispensable to Potiphar. But more trouble was brewing. Unfortunately, the young slave had also caught the eye of Potiphar's wife, who began to repeatedly tempt Joseph to sleep with her. Joseph's response in Genesis 39:8 was very telling:

> *"With me in charge, . . . my master does not concern himself with anything in the house; everything he owns he has entrusted to my care. No one is greater in this house than I am. My master has withheld nothing from me except you, because you are his wife. How then could I do such a wicked thing and sin against God?"*

First, Joseph seemed to be truly thankful to Potiphar for what he had provided. He clearly saw his place and role in the life of his "adopted" family. He knew what had been given to him and he knew his limitations.

Secondly, he feared God. He did not say, "How could I do this to Potiphar?" but rather, "how could I do such a wicked thing and sin against God?" Somewhere along the line, Joseph had recognized God was with him, and his God was to be feared and obeyed. It is a rare thing for a young, virile man to be a God-fearer. Certainly, God would honor those who honored Him, and would reward Joseph for his faithfulness.

But not right away.

Prison – again

It is said that no good deed goes unpunished. When Potiphar's wife's advances were repulsed by Joseph, she turned vindictive and seized him. Joseph ran from the house, and she was left clutching his cloak. Once again, a piece of clothing was going to get Joseph into hot water.

This evil woman concocted a story that Joseph attempted to rape her, and only by screaming for help did she escape. When this news reached Potiphar, he was enraged and threw Joseph into prison. Joseph did not get his day in court – that was not the way justice worked in ancient Egypt.

Once again, Joseph endured a major turn in his life. A modern man could soon develop a strong victim mentality, or become full of bitterness and self-pity:

"What did I do to deserve this?"

"Is this the thanks I get for being a faithful, God-fearing slave to my master?"

He was sent to prison, in a sense, for a second time in his young life – and once again, in a most unjust way. For a second time he was torn from a place of fulfilling activity and contentment in a comfortable household through no fault of his own and plunged again into darkness.

Yet, there is no record of Joseph becoming bitter or angry. All we read in the Genesis account is that *". . . while Joseph was there in prison, the LORD was with him; he showed him kindness and granted him favor in the eyes of the prison warden."* (Genesis 39:20b – 21)

What a remarkable truth – while in prison the Lord was with Joseph. He seemed to be in the center of God's will, although on the surface it appeared that his God had abandoned him.

Like Potiphar, the warden saw Joseph as a great asset in doing his own business. We do not know how long it took, but the young Hebrew was put in charge of all the prisoners and he was given responsibility for all that was done there. In a real sense, here in ancient Egypt the inmates were running the prison. At least one inmate was – namely, Joseph. It seemed that in every situation Joseph found himself, he became a favorite with those in authority. This was because the Lord was with him. He was like a cat always able to land on his feet, no matter what somersaults life threw at him.

A Quick Way Out?

Joseph's amazing story continued there in Pharaoh's jail. His time in prison was not a short sentence. We read, *"Some time later . . . "* (Genesis 40:1), two of Pharaoh's top servants – his cupbearer and cook – are thrown into prison and put in Joseph's care. Then again after they had been in prison *"for some time"* (Genesis 40:4b), both men had dreams on the same night. The men were dejected because they could not figure out what the dreams meant. Joseph was in close proximity to them to see their distress, and he asked them what was troubling them.

They related their dreams to Joseph, who apparently had a God-given knack for interpreting dreams. He predicted two very different futures for the cupbearer and the baker. The cupbearer was to be restored to service of the Pharaoh, while the baker was to be beheaded and hanged. Joseph added a request to his interpretation of the cupbearer's dream in Genesis 40:14.

> *"But when all goes well with you, remember me and show me kindness, mention me to Pharaoh and get me out of this prison. For I was forcibly carried off from the land of the Hebrews, and even here I have done nothing to deserve being put in a dungeon."*

Strangely, this was the only time we see Joseph telling his story. He saw an opportunity for hope and deliverance, and he seized upon it.

Joseph's interpretations of the dreams turned out to be completely accurate. But the cupbearer's memory failed him; he selfishly forgot Joseph. The young Hebrew was so close to getting justice, but because of the thoughtlessness of the cupbearer, he continued to be imprisoned in the dungeon. His tenure in the jail continued for two more years. How patient can an innocent man be? But God intervened with yet another dream.

Pharaoh's Dream

It seems that God sometimes uses dreams to communicate truth and what he wants people to do. This was certainly the case with Pharaoh. He had two successive dreams, and when he awakened the next morning, he was deeply troubled. The dreams must have seemed so real that he knew they were significant. In Genesis 41:8, we read that he sent for his magicians and wise men, but none of them could interpret the dreams' meanings.

Others in Pharaoh's court had been watching this drama unfold. One was an old acquaintance of Joseph's. The chief cupbearer – the former prisoner Joseph had cared for – remembered the young Hebrew who had interpreted his dream accurately while he was in prison. Pharaoh was desperate enough to call for the prisoner. Very quickly Joseph was summoned from the dungeon, cleaned up, and brought before the most powerful man in the ancient world.

Switchbacks

How suddenly things changed for Joseph once again. This time for the better.

"Pharaoh said to Joseph, 'I had a dream, and no one can interpret it. But I have heard it said of you that when you hear a dream you can interpret it.' 'I cannot do it,' Joseph replied to Pharaoh. 'But God will give Pharaoh the answer he desires.'" (Genesis 41:15-16)

Joseph made it clear to Pharaoh his power and ability came from his God. He then went on to interpret Pharaoh's dreams accurately. There was to be a great famine in the entire region – one that would last for seven years. It would be preceded by seven good years of harvest. Such a stretch of bad harvests would not be expected after a long line of good years. Potentially, this could be a disaster for Egypt and the surrounding nations. But like with many disasters, there was also opportunity for growth and strength to emerge through bad times for those who were prepared. Joseph not only interpreted the dreams, but added: *"The reason the dream was given to Pharaoh in two forms is that the matter has been firmly decided by God, and God will do it soon."* (Genesis 41:32)

Joseph's mind jumped ahead to a contingency plan that Pharaoh should embark upon, and he shared his idea. Joseph spoke with such certainty and authority that Pharaoh was impressed. He concluded there was only one man for the job. He immediately appointed Joseph to the top post in his government. He saw wisdom and ability in this young Hebrew prisoner. Much to his credit, Pharaoh acted quickly and decisively.

How remarkable! God moved so quickly and dramatically to establish Joseph in his new royal position after years of languishing unjustly in an Egyptian prison. For many years, God seemed to move hardly at all in helping him, and yet when God did act it was practically in the blink of an eye. Joseph's head must have been reeling with the turn in his fortunes. He was given a signet ring, new fancy clothes (again), a gold chain around his neck, and a chariot. He was also given a new name and an Egyptian wife. He was now thirty years old. Between ages seventeen and thirty, he had lived a life with enough twists and turns to fill an entire lifetime. During the years of rich harvest and storage, Joseph had two sons. His firstborn was Manasseh ("God has made me forget all my trouble and all my father's household"), and Ephraim ("God has made me twice fruitful in the land of my suffering"). He was settling into his new life as an Egyptian transplant.

And as he had in his past positions, Joseph jumped right in and got to work. He showed himself to be completely trustworthy and competent. During the years of plenty, silos were built and storage cities were constructed. Joseph created an efficient infrastructure to store and later distribute grain, further solidifying Egypt's place as the most powerful nation on earth. When the years of famine begin, all people ran to Pharaoh for food, and he sent them to Joseph. He sold grain to them.

Here Come the Brothers

What happened next was predictable. The famine was so severe and widespread that Jacob's entire family felt the pangs of it. They too had to go to Egypt to buy food in order to survive. It appears God's people often had to travel to Egypt as part of the divine plan!

Joseph named his firstborn son Manasseh, which sounds like the Hebrew word for "forget." Joseph was trying to forget his painful past, but God had other plans. Imagine his emotions when ten of his eleven brothers showed up in the food line!

We read that he recognized them right away, but he pretended not to know them and spoke harshly to them. (Genesis 42:7) We also read that the brothers bowed down before Joseph, and he remembered his dreams.

What followed is worthy of a Hollywood script writer. Why did Joseph hide his identity from his brothers for so long, and why did he create such intrigue? It was as if he were playing head games with them! Was he testing the character of his brothers? Was he seeking to determine if they would still betray a brother to benefit themselves? Was he dealing with his own anger and bitterness? There is no clear answer in Scripture, but if Joseph was being led by God in this situation, the brothers experienced some serious zig-zags in their own lives through these encounters with their long-lost brother.

Joseph accused them of being spies, and he tested them. He put them in jail for three days, and then he declared that one brother would stay in jail until their youngest brother Benjamin appeared before him. Upon hearing this plan of the young Egyptian ruler, the brothers conferred with one another, and Joseph overheard their conversation:

> *"Surely we are being punished because of our brother. We saw how distressed he was when he pleaded with us for his life, but we would not listen; that's why this distress has come upon us." (Genesis 42:21)*

Perhaps the brothers were showing true signs of remorse and confession of sin. This touched Joseph to the point where he wept. Brother Simeon was taken and bound before the other brothers' eyes, as Joseph's ruse continued to be played out.

Had Joseph's brothers become honest men? Joseph continued to try to determine this in his own unique and creative way. On their return to Canaan, they discovered their payment of silver had been put back in their grain sacks, much to their dismay. People in Egypt may have thought they were thieves as well as spies. When they got back home, they told their father Jacob the truth (for a change) about all that had happened to them. Jacob believed he had lost yet another son – Simeon this time – and he was adamant he would not part with Benjamin, his youngest son.

A Second Trip to Egypt

The food the brothers purchased in Egypt eventually ran out, because the famine lingered so long. More food had to be obtained, and the brothers knew Benjamin must come with them to Egypt this time. In pleading with their father Jacob to release Benjamin, some remarkable character traits emerged in this family. Reuben and Judah took personal responsibility and vowed to protect their youngest brother. They gave assurances to keep him safe and to return him to his grieving father. It seemed that Joseph's charade had some positive effect after all.

So, the brothers embarked for Egypt a second time, bringing with them double payment for their grain and gifts from Canaan to placate the young Egyptian official. When they arrived, they did not hide anything from the steward about the silver that had been returned to them on their first visit. They openly related the story and offered to return the money. They had come to understand that honesty was the best policy. Their imprisoned brother Simeon was restored to them.

Joseph arranged for the Hebrew entourage to be brought to his house for a banquet. This must have completely surprised the brothers. Why would an Egyptian ruler do this for them? What was going to happen next?

They were treated as honored guests. They were given water to wash their feet and even their donkeys were fed. When Joseph entered, the brothers bowed down to him once more and presented their gifts to him. Upon seeing Benjamin, Joseph was overcome with emotion and left to weep once more. The meal resumed upon his return with the brothers arranged in chronological order at the dinner table. All in all, the meeting was a wonderful experience, and the eleven sons of Jacob all headed back to Canaan with grain for the future.

Benjamin Framed and Joseph Revealed

But Joseph had one more test for his brothers. He framed Benjamin by making it look like the youngest brother had stolen a silver cup from Joseph. What would the older brothers do to protect him? What character would they exhibit when faced with such a crisis? Would they defend Benjamin, or save their own hides?

When confronted, the silver cup was found in Benjamin's possession. All the brothers tore their clothes and returned to Egypt to beg for Benjamin's life. It became clear they were willing to give their own lives for Benjamin and for the well-being of their elderly father. Judah, their spokesman, related their entire family story to Joseph.

Joseph now felt it was the time to end his ruse, and revealed himself to his brothers. Rightly, they were all terrified by his presence and the realization of his true identity. But he reassured them in Genesis 45:4-8.

> *"I am your brother Joseph, the one you sold into Egypt! And now, do not be distressed and do not be angry with yourselves for selling me here, because it was to save lives that God sent me ahead of you. For two years now there has been famine in the land, and for the next five years there will not be plowing and reaping. But God sent me ahead of you to preserve for you a remnant on earth and to save your lives by a great deliverance. So then, it was not you sent me here but God. He made me father to Pharaoh, lord of his entire household and ruler of all Egypt."*

Joseph, perhaps according to God's will, put some zigs and zags in his brother's paths. This helped them come to grips with their sin and shed light on the family secret of what really happened to Joseph. The "Joseph-induced crisis" brought the brothers closer together and also brought out selfless, sacrificial, loving actions – which were noticeably absent years earlier. Joseph's actions also caused them to confess and realize their past sins.

So, Jacob and his clan settled in Egypt and prospered during the famine and beyond. But there was at least one more event that needs to be mentioned. Upon Jacob's death, the brothers were fearful Joseph would take his revenge. Here is where we truly see what was in Joseph's heart.

After their patriarch father was buried, the brothers started with some classic "what if" thinking:

"When Joseph's brothers saw that their father was dead, they said, 'What if Joseph holds a grudge against us and pays us back all the wrongs we did to him?'" (Genesis 50:15)

Joseph, after all, was still the one of the most powerful men in Egypt and had the power to destroy them all. They sent word to Joseph and begged him to forgive them for the sake of their father. When Joseph heard their message, he wept. He reassured his brothers that he would take no revenge. *"You intended to harm me, but God intended it for good...."* (Genesis 50:20a)

What I find most remarkable in this story is that Joseph actually loved his brothers and saw God working behind it all. Joseph was fortunate he lived to see the purpose of his suffering and the culmination of God's ultimate plan for his life. Joseph was one of those rare people in the Bible who lived long enough to see the meaning and destination of his life's winding path. He came to understand why God had done what He had in his life. Many other biblical figures were not so blessed. For Joseph, it appears his toughest years were from age seventeen through thirty-seven. He lived to the age of 110, and we read very little about his last 73 years.

The book of Genesis ends with the death of Joseph. He left clear instructions that he wanted his body buried in Canaan, not Egypt. In the end, he was a Hebrew and identified himself with God's people. And this is what ultimately happened; the book of Joshua ends with the account of Joseph's bones being carried back and buried in the Promised Land. (Joshua 24:32)

The End of the Line

There are many lessons we can take away from the life of Joseph. Here are just a few:

- God used suffering and crooked paths to transform Joseph from a selfish, proud, naïve, "daddy's favorite" into a hard-working, industrious and faithful servant. One can only wonder if Joseph would have developed the skills he did if he had stayed in Canaan and not been uprooted and forced into slavery in Egypt.

- God worked in Joseph's life because He knew a devastating famine was coming – and He had a plan to save his people. It was not the most direct way of doing things, but exceedingly wise and artful nonetheless!

- We see God not only works through individuals, but through families. Joseph was used by God to bring salvation to his extended family. This should be a great comfort to those of us with loved ones not walking with the Lord. God can use individuals to transform, reconcile and redeem entire families.

- The seven-year famine was a big deal – much bigger than we 21st Century Americans can imagine. Joseph's work was cut out for him. Even after he was reconciled to his brothers, it was a mammoth task and he had to work very hard for many years. We sometimes believe if God blesses us, we won't have to work very hard. This was not the case with Joseph, and I suspect it is not the case with us, either.

- Through it all, the Lord was with Joseph. And, like Jesus, Joseph learned obedience through the things that he suffered. (Hebrews 5:8) We do not read about Joseph wallowing in the mire with a victim mentality or growing bitter, frustrated and resentful, demanding justice and deliverance. He "bloomed where he was planted." He did not worry about his rights or not getting what he deserved. "Deserving" had nothing to do with it. In the same way, our lives are not about us, but about God and His plan.

- Joseph actually lived to see what God's plan was for his life. This was a rare gift from God! We do not always see so clearly why God puts us through what He does, but Joseph lived long enough to actually see why God brought him to Egypt: It was to save an entire nation through him. God is working His purpose out, and it may remain hidden from us all our lives. But we can still trust it is a good and perfect plan – one that ultimately brings Him all the glory.

- Joseph languished for many years, and at times it seemed like his lot would never change. Then, in a twinkling of an eye, God acted in a most startling way. When it is time for God to enact change, it can often happen suddenly and unexpectedly. So we should never give up hope when we face tough situations.

The story of Joseph is a testimony to the God of Israel. Even Pharaoh realized early on that Joseph was *"one in whom is the spirit of God."* (Genesis 41:38) God got the glory in Joseph's life, and that is the way it should ultimately be in our lives as well.

Questions for Reflection and Discussion

1. If you were one of Joseph's brothers, how would you have reacted to him at the beginning of this story? Are there any of his traits that would have especially bothered you?

Switchbacks

2. How do you think Joseph avoided becoming bitter and angry in all that he went through? What might your reactions have been to the things he went through if such things happened to you? Who might you have been tempted to be angry with – the brothers? Potiphar's wife? The forgetful wine bearer? God?

3. How do you think the hardships Joseph experienced shaped him into the person he became? How did he avoid falling into having a "victim mentality?"

4. Joseph came to realize his life was not simply about him. How were others affected by the way he lived and the decisions he made? How did his personal journey impact those around him?

5. How do you react to the fact that in every situation in Joseph's life, he was in the center of God's will and plan? How might this truth help you in your difficult circumstances?

6. Have you ever had your circumstances change "in the twinkling of an eye" the way Joseph's did? Were they good or bad changes? Describe such circumstances and how you reacted to them. What might God have been teaching you through such experiences?

7. There are some fascinating similarities between the lives of Jesus and Joseph. Can you name some of them?

David Rox

Switchbacks

4

Falling Off a Cliff: JOB

God is His own interpreter, and He will make it plain.
Hymn by William Cowper, 1774: *God Moves in a Mysterious Way*

Oh, the depth of the riches of the wisdom and knowledge of God! How unsearchable his judgments, and his paths beyond tracing out!
(Romans 11:33)

What do we do when our lives fall off a cliff?

I hesitated including Job in this book, because his story is too much of a "crooked path" to comprehend. This ancient Old Testament book is "the deep end of the pool," as is most of the biblical wisdom literature. The book of Job is not a history or biography; we don't follow the life story of a person. We view him after a cataclysm.

In the first chapter, we meet Job. He was a blameless and upright man who feared God and shunned evil. As we shall see, this is true throughout the story, from first to last. In the beginning, he was a godly man who had it all – the perfect life. He was the greatest and wealthiest man in the East. His seven sons would take turns throwing banquets, inviting friends and their three sisters. As an ancient patriarch of his family, he served as priest for his clan. Job would offer sin offerings just in case they cursed God in their hearts. It seemed this was one of his greatest fears. He not only shunned evil himself, he was concerned about sin in his children's relationship to God – just like godly parents today.

We are then ushered into the throne room of God in heaven. God had a conversation with Satan – a most unusual occurrence in Scripture. The Lord of the universe asked Satan what he had been up to – as if He didn't already know! Satan told God that he had been roaming the earth. And then God brought up the issue of one man: *"Have you considered my servant Job?"* (Job 1:8) God described Job as a blameless and upright man – one who feared God and shunned evil. God almost baited Satan into asking permission to afflict Job, for God even knew what Satan was thinking. Satan took the bait and asked permission to attack Job and his family, and for some hidden, mysterious reason, God gave the go ahead.

Satan was trying to get Job to curse God, and believed that by having him suffer, that was exactly what would happen. If Job cursed God, Satan would win the wager.

Utter Calamity

What follows is a bit more than just a streak of bad luck for Job. In the span of a few minutes, Job's life fell off the table. He lost all his oxen, donkeys, and servants through a Sabean raid. Fire from heaven fell and destroyed more servants and sheep. The Chaldeans raided his property and took all his camels and killed more of his servants. And if this were not enough, a windstorm collapsed the house of Job's oldest son during a family banquet and all his sons and daughters were killed.

Job tore his robe – he realized that such a tidal wave of bad news had to be an act of God. He fell to the ground in worship, and uttered those famous words: *"Naked I came from my mother's womb, and naked I will depart. The LORD gave and the LORD has taken away; may the name of the LORD be praised."* (Job 1:21)

In all this, Job did not curse God. It seemed like God won the wager and Satan had lost.

However, Satan wanted to up the ante. He asked permission to take Job's health away. After all, if you don't have your health, you don't have anything. So, God granted further permission to allow Satan to afflict Job with boils all over his body. He was allowed to do anything to him except to kill him.

After this, Job's wife had had enough. She offered Job two pieces of advice: *"Curse God and die."* (Job 2:9). She broke, but Job stood firm. *"You are talking like a foolish woman. Shall we accept good from God, And not trouble?"* (Job 2:10) Satan seemingly lost round two as well.

Job got hit with everything. Look at what he lost! I have to ask myself, if this were to happen to me, would such events demolish my faith and identity? Yet, Job's tenacity was firm and his faith remained intact – even if he was hanging on for dear life. If all these trials were not enough, things were about to get even worse for him. Enter his three friends Eliphaz, Bildad and Zophar.

With Friends Like These . . .

Upon hearing the news about Job, these three friends met together by agreement to go and sympathize with their poor friend. They truly cared about him and even showed love for him. They also realized what had happened to Job must be an act of God. When they saw Job from a distance, they hardly recognized him. They wept and tore their robes. Then they sat in silence with Job for seven full days.

They should have stayed sitting silently a while longer.

Eliphaz, Bildad and Zophar waited for Job to speak first – that was a kind thing to do. Job was ready to let his feelings out after a week of silence. He began by cursing the day he was born. He did not curse God, but rather, the day of his birth. He was bitter in his soul, and the "whys" began to cascade from his lips.

> *"Why didn't I perish at birth?" (Job 3:11)*
>
> *"Why wasn't I hid in the ground like a stillborn child?" (Job 3;16)*
>
> *"Why is light given to those in misery, and life to the bitter of soul?" (Job 3:20)*

Eliphaz was the first to respond to Job in Chapter 4. He told Job he must be reaping what he had sown: *"As I have observed, those who plow evil and those who sow trouble reap it."* (Job 4:8) Eliphaz showed himself to be a "formula thinker." He believed that he had God all figured out. *"If a person does this, God will obviously do this in response."* How neat and predictable his God was! But are we any different? We want to think we can always have answers for everything that happens in life, don't we?

But Job was not buying it. He knew that God was not punishing him for his sin. He was being *tested*, not punished, and this was a critical distinction. He maintained his innocence and appealed to his friends for mercy:

> *"But now be so kind to look at me. Would I lie to your face? Relent, do not be unjust; reconsider, for my integrity is at stake. Is there any wickedness on my lips? Can my mouth not discern malice?" (Job 6:28-30)*

Friend number two spoke to Job next. Bildad's message was along the same line as Eliphaz's. Bildad had surmised that Job's sons died because they were being punished for their sins. Can you imagine saying such a thing to a grieving father? Yet Bildad believed he was speaking for God. Job's second friend seemed to imply that Job had been a bad father to raise such sinful children.

Bildad's message was the same, ironically, as John the Baptist's: Repent and God will forgive your sins and restore you. It turned out to be a good message at a bad time. Here was how Bildad put it:

> *"How long will you say such things? Your words are like blustering wind. Does God pervert justice? Does the Almighty pervert what is right? When your children sinned against him, he gave them over to the penalty of their sin. But if you look to God and plead with the Almighty, if you are pure and upright, even now he will rouse himself on your behalf and restore you to your rightful place."* (Job 8:2-6)

This was a classic case of a misapplication of God's truth. There is a right time and a wrong time to apply Scripture, and it takes great wisdom to know the difference. Everything Bildad said in his first response to Job was true in itself, but not for Job's situation.

Job said as much in his response to Bildad. *"Indeed, I know that this is true, but how can a man be righteous before God?"* (Job 9:2) Job never claimed to be without sin. But he had an issue with God's justice, and he made it known. He complained about God's seemingly arbitrary actions:

> *"He destroys both the blameless and the wicked. When a scourge brings sudden death, he mocks the despair of the innocent. When a land falls into the hand of the wicked, he blindfolds its judges. If it is not he, then who is it?"* (Job 9:22-24)

Job was asking God, "Why are you throwing *my* sins up in my face, while other more wicked men prosper?" Perhaps this is something we have demanded answers for at some point in our walk with God.

Next, the third friend got into the conversation. Zophar showed himself to be even more of a "formula thinker" than his two friends. He called Job a liar and a mocker of God. *"Is this talker to be vindicated?"* (Job 11:2b) Listen to his message in these following verses from Job 11:14-17. Notice the "if/then" thinking:

> *"If you put away the sin that is in your hand and allow no evil to dwell in your tent, then you will lift up your face without shame; you will stand firm and without fear. You will surely forget your trouble, recalling it only as waters gone by. Life will be brighter than noonday, and darkness will become like morning."*

How presumptuous! Zophar was convinced that Job was guilty of some great sin, so he misapplied spiritual truth to the situation. "If you repent, then you will live happily ever after." While God may act like this in some situations, we cannot demand that He act like this all the time. We do not know all of God's plans or reasons.

Now all three of Job's friends had their first round of verbal sparring with Job. Yet he remained unconvinced by their arguments. He was not buying their explanations for why God had done this to him.

Rounds Two and Three

Job indulged in a little self-pity. Who can blame him? *"I am a laughingstock to my friends, . . . though righteous and blameless."* (Job 12:4) He begged his friends to shut up and to stop attacking him. It was only natural for him to lash out against his friends:

> *"You, however, smear me with lies; you are worthless physicians, all of you! If only you would be altogether silent! For you, that would be wisdom."*
> *(Job 13:4-5)*

From Chapter 15 onward, Job's friends redoubled their corrective efforts, and the conversations got even more heated. And as things got more intense, they became more pointless. No one was going to change anyone's mind in this argument. The three friends said, in short: "God punishes sinners! That's you, Job." Job replied that he knew the arguments, but what he needed was comfort from his friends, not correction.

> *"I also could speak like you, if you were in my place; I could make fine speeches against you and shake my head at you. But my mouth would encourage you; comfort from my lips would bring you relief."* (Job 16:4-5)

Everyone in the story was telling the other person to stop talking. Notice how many of the conversations began this way:

Eliphaz: *"If someone ventures a word with you, will you be impatient?"* (Job 4:2)

Bildad: *"How long will you say such things? Your words are a blustering wind."* (Job 8:2)

Job: *"Will your long-winded speeches never end?"* (Job 16:3)

Bildad: *"When will you end these speeches?"* (Job 18:2)

Job: *"How long will you torment me and crush me with words?"* (Job 19:2)

They were not having a dialogue, but a "dualogue." They were talking past each other. Job was feeling persecuted, while his three friends were feeling dishonored. It was a classic stalemate. What does the book of Proverbs say about too many words? *"Sin is not ended by multiplying words, but the prudent hold their tongues."* (Proverbs 10:19)

Job wanted comforting, and the friends wanted Job to accept their explanation for why he was suffering. The friends presumed they knew the mind of God, and they were terribly wrong. The presumptuousness of Job's friends came to its apex when Eliphaz groundlessly accuses Job of specific sins:

> *"Is not your wickedness great? Are not your sins endless? You demanded security from your relatives for no reason; you stripped people of their clothing, leaving them naked.*
>
> *You gave no water to the weary and you withheld food from the hungry, though you were a powerful man, owning land — an honored man, living on it. And you sent widows away empty-handed and broke the strength of the fatherless.*
>
> *That is why snares are all around you, why sudden peril terrifies you, Why it is so dark you cannot see, and why a flood of water covers you." (Job 22:5-11)*

His formula for Job's relief is restated yet again: *"Submit to God and be at peace with him; in this way prosperity will come to you.* (Job 22:21)

The third round of debate ended. More heat had been generated than light. Two of the three friends have had three tries, and poor Zophar stopped at two rounds because he had no more to say.

Job Files Suit

Who did Job blame for his situation? Does he blame Satan? His sin? His family? His friends? No, he blames God. And rightly so!

Job wanted to argue his case before God. He also wanted answers as to why he was being tormented in such horrific ways. He asked God for two things: for God to cease and desist and to give him his day in court.

> *"Only grant me these two things, O God, and then I will not hide from you: withdraw your hand far from me, and stop frightening me with your terrors. Then summon me and I will answer, or let me speak and you reply." (Job 13:20–22)*

In modern days, Job might file a restraining order and an anti-discrimination suit against the Almighty. It was very clear in Job's lamenting that he put the blame on God.

"Surely, O God, you have worn me out; you have devastated my entire household." (Job 16:7)

"All was well with me, but he shattered me; he seized me by the neck and crushed me." (Job 16:12)

We really see Job clearly blaming God in chapter 19:7-12

"Though I cry, 'Violence!' I get no response; though I call for help, there is no justice. He has blocked my way so I cannot pass; he has shrouded my paths in darkness. He has stripped me of my honor and removed the crown from my head. He tears me down on every side till I am gone; he uproots my hope like a tree. His anger burns against me; he counts me among his enemies. His troops advance in force; they build a siege ramp against me and encamp around my tent."

Job had issues with God's justice – or lack thereof. God did not punish all the wicked in their lifetimes. Many lived happy lives while many righteous people suffered. This was unjust. Job and other righteous people did not deserve to suffer. What about their rights?

His words to his three friends were clear:

"I will never admit you are in the right; till I die, I will not deny my integrity. I will maintain my innocence and never let go of it; my conscience will not reproach me as long as I live." (Job 27:5-6)

On top of all Job's sufferings, God inflicted Job with silence. He got no answers from God for a long, long time. If ever a man searched for God and could not find him, it was Job. *"If only I knew where to find him; if only I could go to his dwelling!"* (Job 23:3) If Job could have found God, he could have presented his innocence to him and God would clear him of all charges. But the Almighty was nowhere to be found. Silence from God can be a terribly hard thing to endure. I think of the old song by Simon and Garfunkle. *The Sounds of Silence* – "Hello darkness, my old friend." There is a darkness about silence – especially silence from God. Why does God sometimes leave us in darkness?

In Chapter 31, Job outlined his innocence in great detail, and prepared his case to present before God. He maintained that he was a man who had feared God and shunned evil. His point was simply that God is not punishing him for sin, but rather inflicting him with suffering for no apparent reason.

There is one more friend to speak to Job before the story ends – enter Elihu.

The Young Man Elihu

A rather mysterious latecomer entered the story at this point. A young man named Elihu had been an observer of all these proceedings. He had held his tongue out of respect for his elders, but now he was angry and ready to speak on behalf of God. We read that he was angry at Job for justifying himself rather than God, and angry at the three friends because they could not refute Job, yet they condemned him. (Job 32:2-3) His argument with Job took a different tack than previous ones. He took issue with Job's claim of innocence before God. Elihu shows some wisdom in that he focuses on God's sovereignty.

> *"Why do you complain to him that he answers none of man's words? For God does speak – now one way, now another – though man may not perceive it." (Job 33:13-14)*

The young man reminded Job he could not put God on trial, and all men were sinners, when all was said and done. There was some wisdom in what Elihu said. When God finally appeared, Elihu was the only friend of Job who was not condemned for his words. Job had to remember that his life was not about having his rights upheld or getting what he deserved. His life was about God and his glory. Elihu outlined many of God's wonders, foreshadowing what God himself said later on.

> *"Listen to this, Job; stop and consider God's wonders. Do you know how God controls the clouds and makes his lightning flash? Do you know how the clouds hang poised, those wonders of him who has perfect knowledge?*
>
> *You who swelter in your clothes when the land lies hushed under the south wind, can you join him in spreading out the skies, hard as a mirror of cast bronze?*
>
> *"Tell us what we should say to him; we cannot draw up our case because of our darkness. Should he be told that I want to speak? Would anyone ask to be swallowed up?*
>
> *Now no one can look at the sun, bright as it is in the skies after the wind has swept them clean. Out of the north he comes in golden splendor; God comes in*

> *awesome majesty. The Almighty is beyond our reach and exalted in power; in his justice and great righteousness, he does not oppress.*
>
> *Therefore, people revere him, for does he not have regard for all the wise in heart?" (Job 37:14-24)*

Elihu was more God-focused than Job-focused – he spoke not of what Job had done wrong, but more of who God was. Much earlier in the story, Job had said, *"The LORD gave and the LORD has taken away; may the name of the LORD be praised."* (Job 1:21b) Elihu was pretty much saying the same thing, reminding Job of this truth. Job did not get a chance to answer Elihu – God interrupted. As the old hymn reminds us: "God is His own interpreter, and He will make it plain."

God Finally Speaks!

It is said that once a Gentile asked a rabbi, "Why is it that you Jewish teachers always answer people's questions with another question?"

The rabbi replied, "Why not?"

Up to this point, one of Job's main questions for God was, "Where are you?" In modern terms, Job wished to file an anti-discrimination suit against God – a cease and desist order. Job wanted his day in court. He complained that God had been unjust, and Job was in the right.

Well, God finally did speak to Job, and in some ways his message was more terrifying than all Job had endured up to this point. In true rabbinic fashion, God began his answer to Job by asking a slightly different, more basic question of the man. Instead of God answering, "Where are you?" he asks Job, "Where were you?" Or another way of saying it: "Who do you think you are?"

> *"Where were you when I laid the earth's foundation? Tell me, if you understand." (Job 38:4)*

This penetrating question set the tone for all that God had to say. He told Job to brace himself like a man, because God was about to question him and he would have to answer. In truth, God did not have to answer Job, but Job would have to answer God.

What followed was a series of rhetorical questions that Job could not possibly answer – only God knew the answers. Here is just a small sample of the questions on God's quiz for Job:

> "Have you ever given orders to the morning, or shown the dawn its place, that it might take the earth by the edges and shake the wicked out of it?" (Job 38:12-13)
>
> "Have you journeyed to the springs of the sea, or walked in the recesses of the deep?" (Job 38:16)
>
> "Have the gates of death been shown to you? Have you seen the gates of the shadow of death?" (Job 38:17)
>
> "Can you bind the beautiful Pleiades? Can you loose the cords of Orion?" (Job 38:31)
>
> "Do you send the lightning bolts on their way? Do they report to you, 'Here we are?'" (Job 38:35)
>
> "Do you give the horse his strength, or clothe his neck with a flowing mane?" (Job 39:19)
>
> "Will the one who contends with the Almighty correct him? Let him who accuses God answer him." (Job 40:2)

Halfway through the quiz, Job answered the Lord:

> "I am unworthy – how can I reply to you? I put my hand over my mouth. I spoke once, but I have no answer – twice, but I will say no more." (Job 40:4-5)

But God was not done. His daunting barrage of questions continued, and the really hard questions were yet to come.

> "Brace yourself like a man; I will question you, and you shall answer me. "Would you discredit my justice? Would you condemn me to justify yourself?
>
> Do you have an arm like God's, and can your voice thunder like his? Then adorn yourself with glory and splendor, and clothe yourself in honor and majesty.
>
> Unleash the fury of your wrath, look at all who are proud and bring them low, look at all who are proud and humble them, crush the wicked where they stand.
>
> Bury them all in the dust together; shroud their faces in the grave. Then I myself will admit to you that your own right hand can save you. (Job 40:7-14)

Implied in God's questioning is that He alone knew the answers. God even shared many examples of his vast knowledge in his discourse.

When the quiz is finally over, Job replies to the Lord:

> "I know that you can do all things; no purpose of yours can be thwarted. You asked, 'Who is this that obscures my plans without knowledge?' Surely I spoke of things I did not understand, things too wonderful for me to know.
>
> "You said, 'Listen now, and I will speak; I will question you, and you shall answer me.' My ears had heard of you but now my eyes have seen you. Therefore I despise myself and repent in dust and ashes." (Job 42:2-6)

Job did not get his questions answered. Instead he caught a glimpse of the greatness of God himself, which in the end was more than sufficient to satisfy his soul.

The End of the Line

In the epilogue of this great book, we read that God straightened things out. He called for repentance on the part of Job's three friends, who had mistreated Job. They repented and Job prayed for them. These relationships were restored. After this, God blessed Job. He was healed of his afflictions, blessed with wealth and family once again – even beyond what he originally had. Truly, "the Lord gave and the Lord took away; blessed be the name of the Lord."

But the ending of the story is really not the point. Here are some critical "takeaways" from this story:

- The message of Job is not that if you hang in there long enough, God will deliver you. We should not be guilty of this kind of simplistic "formula thinking." The happily ever after ending is not the message. On judgment day, all restraining orders and anti-discrimination suits filed against God will be thrown out of court. God has his reasons. He is God and we are not. We may not get our questions about injustice answered. But we will see God, and that is all that will really matter.

- Even a godly person – one who fears God and shuns evil – can be brought to a place where he or she lashes out at God. Such a person may feel like filing suit against God. But God is gracious in such instances and will ultimately show more of Himself.

- Silence from God can be a terrible thing to endure. God has His reasons for remaining silent for a time. Like Job, we have things to learn during silence and waiting upon God.

- Job's friends were narrow thinkers. They thought they had God completely figured out. They stand as a warning to us; we should humbly realize that we do not know all the ways of God, and we should put away all such presumptions. In times of difficulty, we would do well to remember that God is God, and has his reasons for what happens in our lives – even when hidden from us. And when helping our friends through difficult times, we should do far more listening than talking. Job's friends got into trouble when they opened their mouths, and this is often true for us as well.

I am reminded of an old friend's story. My friend Hank was just finishing seminary. He felt God had called him into the ministry. Just as he was graduating, Hank received a terrible diagnosis – he had a serious form of cancer and it was quite advanced. Naturally, he was shocked and perplexed. While painting the side of a house, he began to angrily jab the paint brush into the clapboards and ask God why. *"Why am I being afflicted at this point in time with such a disease – now that I am ready to embark upon a ministry to serve you?"*

Hank once told me, "Dave, I can show you the place on the side of the house where God answered me. When he did answer me, He simply said, *'I have my reasons.'*"

God spoke to him, and his answer really wasn't much of an answer on the surface. But it was all Hank got, and it was all he needed.

Hank was eventually miraculously healed and lived another 25 years. During his remaining years, he had a special ministry to those suffering with cancer. God had his reasons, but they were not readily apparent for many years.

One old Puritan prayer includes the statement: "Lawful blessings are the secret idols, and do most hurt; the greatest injury is in the having, the greatest good is in the taking away."[1] There is wisdom there!

And the last word should go to C.S. Lewis, as he wrote in *Till We Have Faces*:

> "I know now, Lord, why you utter no answer. You are yourself the answer. Before your face questions die away. What other answer would suffice?" [2]

At this, Job would probably say, "Amen."

Questions for Reflection and Discussion

1. Job's life completely fell apart. His loss of family, possessions, and health all hit him in short order. If these things were to happen to you, which would be the hardest for you to bear? How might you react?

2. Job's friends were compassionate at first and came to him, sitting in silence with him for seven days. Have you ever struggled to keep silent when ministering to a friend who is suffering? When is silence a good thing? Why do we feel the need to say something and to break the silence?

3. Job's friends were guilty of "formula thinking" – of believing they had all the answers to life's toughest questions. How might we be guilty of similar thinking when faced with helping a friend through tough times? What does this say about our view of God and how we think He works?

4. Job sat for a long time waiting to hear from God, but was met with silence. Have you ever sensed that God was silent in your life? What can we learn through such times?

5. How do you feel about Job blaming God for all his afflictions? Have you ever lashed out at God and accused Him for your troubles? Can this in any way be a good thing?

6. Job kept going to God, even when met with silence and no answers to his questions. Have you ever really wanted answers from God, and did not get them? How did you react when this happened?

7. What was God's ultimate answer to Job? Might this be His answer to you as well?

David Rox

Switchbacks

5

The Wilderness Way: MOSES

"I have seen these people . . . and they are a stiff-necked people." (Exodus 32:9)

You think your job is a headache? Try pastoring a nomadic megachurch for four decades.

Few people in the history of the world have had a heavier workload than Moses. And few have been more used by God. Moses' life journey was literally one large zig-zag — especially while he led God's reluctant and rebellious people through the wilderness for forty years.

Born and Raised in Egypt

At the start of Moses' story, there were 600,000 Israelites, and they had been in Egypt for 420 years. In the "post-Joseph" generations, all that Joseph had done to save Egypt had been forgotten, and his descendants had begun to be oppressed. Yet they grew in number at an astounding rate. This troubled the new Pharaoh, so he devised a plan: slave labor. Taskmasters afflicted the Hebrews with burdens and they groaned under the load.

And still they increased in number. So, Pharaoh hit upon another solution: infanticide. All the male newborns were to be thrown into the Nile. From the moment Moses was born, his life was in grave danger. The story of how he was rescued and raised is nothing short of miraculous, which is why it is part of "Sunday School legend." This story has been retold on film by everyone from Cecil B. DeMille to Walt Disney. Moses was placed (rather than thrown) into the Nile in a basket by his mother, watched over by his sister Miriam from a distance, and found and eventually raised by Pharaoh's daughter as a prince of Egypt. Like his ancestor Joseph, Moses seemed to have landed on top in Egypt by a remarkable twist of fate.

But Moses knew he was a Hebrew, and he saw the suffering of his people. One day he saw an Egyptian foreman beating a Hebrew slave, and he lost it. We read in Exodus 2 that Moses' solution to this injustice was to kill the Egyptian for his cruelty. So, Moses decided to chart out his own straight path, and took justice into his own hands. This man had a temper, and he was to struggle with it his entire life.

His crime soon became known and Moses had to flee for his life. He ran to Midian, where he settled down in the house of Jethro, married one of his daughters, and started a family. Already he had experienced three cultural changes: from Hebrew to Egyptian to fugitive in Midian. That was surely enough twists and turns for one lifetime. But much more was to come.

The Burning Bush

By Exodus Chapter 3, Moses was already settling down into a comfortable routine. He was approaching his 80th birthday. God was about to teach this "old dog" many new tricks.

God called Moses from a burning bush in the middle of an ordinary workday. Like His call of Abraham long ago, God told Moses to leave and go.

> *The LORD said, "I have indeed seen the misery of my people in Egypt. I have heard them crying out because of their slave drivers, and I am concerned about their suffering. So I have come down to rescue them from the hand of the Egyptians and to bring them up out of that land into a good and spacious land, a land flowing with milk and honey—the home of the Canaanites, Hittites, Amorites, Perizzites, Hivites and Jebusites. And now the cry of the Israelites has reached me, and I have seen the way the Egyptians are oppressing them. So now, go. I am sending you to Pharaoh to bring my people the Israelites out of Egypt." (Exodus 3:7-10)*

Moses was being sent back into a dangerous and difficult situation, and he had objections. Lots of them. *"Who am I?" "Suppose I go and they ask me who you are? What shall I say to them?" "What if they do not believe me?" "Lord, I am not a public speaker. Please send somebody else."*

But God insisted, and Moses had to obey. He was to become the reluctant leader of Israel. And strangely enough, one of the greatest leaders the world has ever known. I am reminded what Shakespeare wrote in *Twelfth Night*: "Be not afraid of greatness; some are born great, some achieve greatness, and some have greatness thrust upon them." God saw something in Moses the man himself did not see. God had thrust greatness upon Moses.

Back to Pharaoh's Court

Moses was about to embark upon a long ordeal with Pharaoh and the people of Israel. Along the way, there would be innumerable roadblocks, apparent detours, failures, discouragements and dangers. The first occurred on his way back to Egypt. In Exodus 4, God was about to kill Moses because he had not circumcised his son. His wife Zipporah performed the act just in time. Moses had to live in obedience in his personal life before he could be God's representative to others.

Moses began to lobby Pharaoh, and the results were not initially successful. His first appeal to Pharaoh resulted in harsher work conditions for all Israel – they were subsequently forced to make bricks without straw. Like in the story of Job, troubles escalated for Moses over time. God's plan was unfolding in a rather baffling manner. It became clear to everyone involved that if God were going to deliver the people of Israel from Egypt, it would not be without a fight. And it would require a series of miraculous signs – each sign more fantastic than the one before.

Water turned into blood. Frogs covered the ground. Gnats. Flies. Death of livestock. Boils on the skin. A destructive hailstorm. Devouring locusts. Unexplained darkness. All of these nearly destroyed the glory of Egypt, yet Pharaoh's heart remained unmoved. Moses was God's messenger of judgment again and again; he was gaining valuable experience listening to God and relaying God's message to others. And he was seeing how powerful his God was, and how utterly reliable His promises were.

It is in this part of the story we see Moses had a unique relationship with God. The pages of Exodus are full of the phrase, "The Lord said to Moses." The Lord spoke to Moses on a regular basis – directly! And often, God told him what was about to happen. And it was rarely good news. Notice how often in these passages God foretold the resistance to Moses' message and mission.

> *The LORD said to Moses, "When you return to Egypt, see that you perform before Pharaoh all the wonders I have given you the power to do. But I will harden his heart so that he will not let the people go. Then say to Pharaoh, 'This is what the LORD says: Israel is my firstborn son, and I told you, "Let my son go, so he may worship me." But you refused to let him go; so I will kill your firstborn son.'" (Exodus 4:21-23)*

> *"Then the Lord said to Moses, 'See, I have made you like God to Pharaoh, and your brother Aaron will be your prophet. You are to say everything I command you, and your brother Aaron is to tell Pharaoh to let the Israelites go out of his*

country. But I will harden Pharaoh's heart, and though I multiply my signs and wonders in Egypt, he will not listen to you. Then I will lay my hand on Egypt and with mighty acts of judgment I will bring out my divisions, my people the Israelites. And the Egyptians will know that I am the LORD when I stretch out my hand against Egypt and bring the Israelites out of it.'" (Exodus 7:1-5)

"Then the Lord said to Moses, 'Go to Pharaoh, for I have hardened his heart and the hearts of his officials so that I may perform these signs of mine among them that you may tell your children and grandchildren how I dealt harshly with the Egyptians and how I performed my signs among them, and that you may know that I am the LORD.'" (Exodus 10:1-2)

God had told Moses again and again that it would be tough, but He would be with him. Forewarned is forearmed.

Passover and the Crossing

Nine horrible plagues had been inflicted upon the Egyptians. Plague number ten would be the last. In Exodus 12, we read the story of the first Passover. God gave His people explicit instructions as to how to prepare for their ultimate deliverance from Egypt and slavery. It involved blood on the doorposts, a hasty meal, and preparations to move quickly into the unknown. God struck a terrible blow on all Egypt by killing the firstborn. Finally, Pharaoh relented and let the Hebrews go.

I find it interesting that after so much time of waiting, and seeing events unfold so slowly through all the previous plagues, finally things unfolded almost at light speed. It is reminiscent of how quickly Joseph was elevated to his position of authority in Egypt by Pharaoh after years of suffering in prison. When God said it was time, there was no more delay. Moses and the Israelites took off quickly after waiting for deliverance a very long time. They were fleeing in haste and heading for freedom.

If I were in the midst of all this turmoil, I might now expect God to resolve things quickly and with finality: *"We have suffered for so long, and finally the Egyptians have let us go. God has performed mighty miracles for us. Now He will lead us to safety and into the Promised Land! It is only a matter of getting there."*

This was hardly the case.

We read in Exodus 13:17 that when Pharaoh let the people go, God did not lead them to the Promised Land by the most direct route, but rather by the desert road toward the Red Sea. God led them with a pillar of cloud by day and a pillar of fire by night. But he did not lead them in a straight path to Canaan.

God had warned Moses ahead of time that Pharaoh would change his mind yet again, and there would be another confrontation. But God would deliver His people and gain glory for His name. God showed His grace to Moses by telling him of the crisis coming, so he was prepared and not panic-stricken when these events unfolded.

Sure enough, Pharaoh had once again changed his mind and his army was thundering toward them with revenge and slaughter on their minds. The people of Israel did what we would have done – they panicked. And they decided to turn on their leader.

> *They said to Moses, "Was it because there were no graves in Egypt that you brought us to the desert to die? What have you done to us by bringing us out of Egypt? Didn't we say to you in Egypt, 'Leave us alone; let us serve the Egyptians'? It would have been better for us to serve the Egyptians than to die in the desert!" (Exodus 14:11-12)*

If Moses was at first a reluctant leader, the people of Israel were consistently reluctant followers. But Moses stood firm. We know the rest of the story. The people crossed the Red Sea in miraculous fashion on dry land. The Egyptians followed but were drowned in the waters.

> *"And when the Israelites saw the mighty hand of the LORD displayed against the Egyptians, the people feared the LORD and put their trust in him and in Moses his servant." (Exodus 14:31)*

God performed a great miracle and the people of God praised Him in celebration and song.

Off to Sinai

Life in the wilderness was perilous. Where could you find water and food for 600,000 people? For three days after the miracle at the Red Sea, they traveled without finding water. And when they finally found water at Marah, it was bitter. The people grumbled against Moses. *"What are we to drink?"* (Exodus 15:24) This grumbling became a habit among the people of Israel. After all, unrest and whining in tough times are part of human nature. And Moses was the brunt of all the grumbling. Yet God graciously provided water for the people at Marah and again at Elim.

No sooner had the water crisis been solved that a food crisis arose. In the Desert of Sin, the people grumbled against Moses again:

> *The Israelites said, "If only we had died by the LORD's hand in Egypt! There we sat around pots of meat and ate all the food we wanted, but you have brought us out into this desert to starve this entire assembly to death." (Exodus 16:3)*

Poor Moses! This is the thanks he got for helping deliver his people. In response, God provided manna for the people to eat – bread from heaven. And because they complained about having no meat, God provided innumerable quail for them as well.

God continued to lead his people through the wilderness to Sinai. On the way, there were battles with the Amalekites and unending disputes that Moses had to settle. His workload was enormous. He was confronted by a remarkable and wise man – his own father-in-law!

> *When his father-in-law saw all that Moses was doing for the people, he said, "What is this you are doing for the people? Why do you alone sit as judge, while all these people stand around you from morning till evening?"*
>
> *Moses answered him, "Because the people come to me to seek God's will. Whenever they have a dispute, it is brought to me, and I decide between the parties and inform them of God's decrees and instructions."*
>
> *Moses' father-in-law replied, "What you are doing is not good. You and these people who come to you will only wear yourselves out. The work is too heavy for you; you cannot handle it alone. Listen now to me and I will give you some advice, and may God be with you. You must be the people's representative before God and bring their disputes to him. Teach them his decrees and instructions, and show them the way they are to live and how they are to behave. But select capable men from all the people—men who fear God, trustworthy men who hate dishonest gain—and appoint them as officials over thousands, hundreds, fifties and tens. Have them serve as judges for the people at all times, but have them bring every difficult case to you; the simple cases they can decide themselves. That will make your load lighter, because they will share it with you. If you do this and God so commands, you will be able to stand the strain, and all these people will go home satisfied." (Exodus 18:14-23)*

If not for Jethro who taught Moses the art of delegation, he probably would have collapsed from exhaustion and complete burnout. Jethro was one of the great unsung heroes in Moses' life.

After three months of travel, the people arrived at Sinai. Here more than at any other time do we see Moses' unique relationship to God. He alone went up the mountain to be with God face to face. He received God's laws for the people and faithfully related them to one and all. These laws became the glue that held the Hebrews together. Not only did Moses present the Ten Commandments, but outlined a legal code of social conduct and regulations for how and where God was to be worshipped. The Ark of the Covenant. The Tabernacle. The priestly role of the Levites. The annual festival celebrations. Laws of social justice. All this and much more was brought to Israel by God through His servant Moses.

Through him, the people of Israel were to become a theocracy.

The Golden Calf

The next chapter of Moses' life was about to begin. The Egyptian threat was part of their past. Moses was pastoring the largest nomadic church in history, and he found out how tough of a job it was.

Problems began almost immediately, right at the foot of Mount Sinai, where God had called his people to worship Him. Moses had been gone atop the mountain for such a long time, the people wondered what had happened to him. The people were there to worship, and they wanted to get on with it. Aaron bent to their pressure and made them a god to worship – a golden calf forged from the plunder the people of Israel took from the Egyptians. Aaron decided to forge his own straight path to solve the problem of Moses' absence. Bad idea! God was about to give the people regulations for worship through Moses, but the people decided to take a short cut.

The resulting celebration quickly became a debauched riot. The people were out of control in their revelry. God warned Moses while he was still up the mountain that the people had sinned.

> *Then the LORD said to Moses, "Go down, because your people, whom you brought up out of Egypt, have become corrupt. They have been quick to turn away from what I commanded them and have made themselves an idol cast in the shape of a calf. They have bowed down to it and sacrificed to it and have said, 'These are your gods, Israel, who brought you up out of Egypt.'*

> *"I have seen these people,"* the LORD said to Moses, *"and they are a stiff-necked people. Now leave me alone so that my anger may burn against them and that I may destroy them. Then I will make you into a great nation."*
> *(Exodus 32:7-10)*

Moses had been gone from camp for what seemed like an eternity for the people of Israel. Yet God said that the people were "quick to turn away." God's idea of time and ours are obviously not the same. God purposed in His heart to destroy them all, but Moses interceded, like a priest for his people.

> *But Moses sought the favor of the LORD his God.*
>
> *"LORD," he said, "why should your anger burn against your people, whom you brought out of Egypt with great power and a mighty hand? Why should the Egyptians say, 'It was with evil intent that he brought them out, to kill them in the mountains and to wipe them off the face of the earth'? Turn from your fierce anger; relent and do not bring disaster on your people. Remember your servants Abraham, Isaac and Israel, to whom you swore by your own self: 'I will make your descendants as numerous as the stars in the sky and I will give your descendants all this land I promised them, and it will be their inheritance forever.'" Then the LORD relented and did not bring on his people the disaster he had threatened. (Exodus 32:11–14)*

So, Moses descended from the Mount with God's commandments etched on stone tablets. When Moses saw the chaos and pagan worship, he lost his cool and smashed the tablets God had written upon. Remember, this man had a temper. The first thing he had to do was to get their attention and distract them from their pagan rioting. He punished the people severely for their sin, pulverizing the golden calf and mixing it with water and making the people drink it, and then calling some of his fellow Levites to kill 3,000 of their kinsmen.

After inflicting this punishment, Moses once again chose to intercede for his people before God.

> *The next day Moses said to the people, "You have committed a great sin. But now I will go up to the LORD; perhaps I can make atonement for your sin."*
>
> *So Moses went back to the LORD and said, "Oh, what a great sin these people have committed! They have made themselves gods of gold. But now, please forgive their sin—but if not, then blot me out of the book you have written."*

The LORD replied to Moses, "Whoever has sinned against me I will blot out of my book. Now go, lead the people to the place I spoke of, and my angel will go before you. However, when the time comes for me to punish, I will punish them for their sin."

And the LORD struck the people with a plague because of what they did with the calf Aaron had made. (Exodus 32:30-35)

Despite all the trouble his people had caused him, Moses had deep love for them all. He was willing to be condemned in their stead, making atonement for them. But if Moses thought the golden calf incident would cure the people of their wayward ways, he was sorely mistaken.

Opposition

Moses had a special relationship with God – perhaps like no other human being has had. He used to have a tent he pitched outside of camp that came to be known as the Tent of Meeting. *"The LORD would speak to Moses face to face, as a man speaks with his friend."* (Exodus 33:11) God even showed Moses all his goodness and glory. (Exodus 33:19-20) Moses' face used to shine after being in God's presence – so much so that the people were afraid to approach him. (Exodus 34:30) He covered his face with a veil so the people could bear to look at him. You would think with these credentials, Moses' leadership would be unchallenged.

Yet we read time and time again that the people grumbled against Moses. He had a rebellion on his hands at least a dozen times. One account given in Numbers 12 probably involved racial bigotry and opposition from his own brother and sister.

Miriam and Aaron began to talk against Moses because of his Cushite wife, for he had married a Cushite. "Has the LORD spoken only through Moses?" they asked. "Hasn't he also spoken through us?" And the LORD heard this. (Numbers 12:1-2)

Moses' siblings seem to have had an inflated opinion of themselves. Perhaps at the root of the problem was jealousy. Miriam and Aaron were jealous of Moses' unique relationship with God. Political intrigue was not something invented in modern times! The Lord set them straight.

At once the LORD said to Moses, Aaron and Miriam, "Come out to the tent of meeting, all three of you." So the three of them went out. Then the Lord came

> *down in a pillar of cloud; he stood at the entrance to the tent and summoned Aaron and Miriam. When the two of them stepped forward, he said, "Listen to my words:*
>
> *"When there is a prophet among you, I, the LORD, reveal myself to them in visions, I speak to them in dreams. But this is not true of my servant Moses; he is faithful in all my house. With him I speak face to face, clearly and not in riddles; he sees the form of the LORD. Why then were you not afraid to speak against my servant Moses?" The anger of the LORD burned against them, and he left them. (Numbers 12:4-9)*

God punished Miriam by inflicting her with leprosy for seven days.

A larger rebellion occurred in Numbers 16. Over 250 well-known community leaders rose up against Moses and Aaron, led by Korah, Dathan and Abiram. They objected to the exclusivity of their priestly roles.

> *"They came as a group to Moses and Aaron and said to them, 'You have gone too far! The whole community is holy, every one of them, and the LORD is with them. Why then do you set yourselves above the LORD's assembly?'" (Numbers 16:3)*

Their insolence and false piety escalated to the point where God opened the earth and swallowed up the rebels alive, along with their households and possessions. They were gone from the face of the earth.

> *Seeing this, the whole Israelite community grumbled against Moses and Aaron. "You have killed the LORD's people." (Numbers 16:41)*

So the Lord followed this up with a plague that killed another 14,700 people. The devastation probably would have been greater if not for the intercession of Moses and Aaron on the people's behalf.

God decided to put an end to the constant grumbling against Moses and Aaron. In Numbers 17 he instructed Moses to have the people bring 12 staffs to the Tent of Meeting – one for each of the twelve tribes of Israel. Overnight, Aaron's staff alone blossomed and budded. This became a sign that God had chosen the house of Levi alone to be priests for the people.

Modern day pastors and Christian leaders would do well to study Moses' life when they feel their congregations cause them headaches. Such troubles are nothing new. In fact, our troubles are minor compared to those of Moses.

Faithlessness

The greatest disappointment in Moses' life had to be when he sent the spies into the land of Canaan. They were poised to enter the Promised Land, on the cusp of the fulfillment of God's plan. But the faithlessness of the leaders snatched defeat out of the jaws of victory.

> *The LORD said to Moses, "Send some men to explore the land of Canaan, which I am giving to the Israelites. From each ancestral tribe send one of its leaders." So at the LORD's command Moses sent them out from the Desert of Paran. All of them were leaders of the Israelites. (Numbers 13:1-3)*

Shammua, Shaphat, Caleb, Igal, Joshua, Palti, Gaddiel, Gaddi, Ammiel, Sethur, Nahbi, and Guel were all leaders of the people. They were supposedly trustworthy men sent to explore the land. You might notice that we hardly remember 10 of the 12 men listed. They returned after 40 days with their news. They all agreed the land was bountiful and attractive in every way. However, the vast majority of the spies focused on the invincibility of the inhabitants, and gave a pessimistic report. They believed there was no way the people of Israel could conquer the land. Joshua and Caleb alone stated, *"We should go up and take possession of the land, for we can certainly do it."* (Numbers 13:30)

Sadly, the majority opinion ruled. Upon hearing the bad report, the people wept aloud.

> *All the Israelites grumbled against Moses and Aaron, and the whole assembly said to them, "If only we had died in Egypt! Or in this wilderness! Why is the LORD bringing us to this land only to let us fall by the sword? Our wives and children will be taken as plunder. Wouldn't it be better for us to go back to Egypt?" And they said to each other, "We should choose a leader and go back to Egypt." (Numbers 14: 2-4)*

Joshua and Caleb pleaded with the people to reconsider:

> *"The land we passed through and explored is exceedingly good. If the LORD is pleased with us, he will lead us into that land, a land flowing with milk and honey, and will give it to us. Only do not rebel against the LORD. And do not be afraid of the people of the land, because we will devour them. Their protection is gone, but the LORD is with us. Do not be afraid of them." (Numbers 14:7-9)*

Instead of rallying behind this stirring speech, this group of "stiff-necked people" talked of stoning Joshua and Caleb to death! But God intervened once again. Few things anger God more than a lack of faith in Him. Once again, He was poised to wipe out the entire nation and make a greater nation of Moses and his descendants. But Moses pleaded for forgiveness, and the Lord relented.

Although God forgave their sin of unbelief, there were consequences.

> *The LORD said to Moses and Aaron: "How long will this wicked community grumble against me? I have heard the complaints of these grumbling Israelites. So tell them, 'As surely as I live, declares the LORD, I will do to you the very thing I heard you say: In this wilderness your bodies will fall—every one of you twenty years old or more who was counted in the census and who has grumbled against me. Not one of you will enter the land I swore with uplifted hand to make your home, except Caleb son of Jephunneh and Joshua son of Nun. As for your children that you said would be taken as plunder, I will bring them in to enjoy the land you have rejected. But as for you, your bodies will fall in this wilderness. Your children will be shepherds here for forty years, suffering for your unfaithfulness, until the last of your bodies lies in the wilderness. For forty years—one year for each of the forty days you explored the land—you will suffer for your sins and know what it is like to have me against you.' I, the LORD, have spoken, and I will surely do these things to this whole wicked community, which has banded together against me. They will meet their end in this wilderness; here they will die." (Numbers 14:26-35)*

So, the trek to the Promise Land for that generation became a prison sentence. Faithlessness led to 40 years of wandering in the wilderness. Here was a case where God was ready to have His people walk a straight path, but their sin and unbelief created great hardship, heartache and a tragic detour. Especially for Moses.

Unfulfilled Dreams

While continuing their wanderings in the Desert of Zin, the people once again grumbled about not having water.

> *They quarreled with Moses and said, "If only we had died when our brothers fell dead before the LORD! Why did you bring the LORD's community into this wilderness, that we and our livestock should die here? Why did you bring us up*

out of Egypt to this terrible place? It has no grain or figs, grapevines or pomegranates. And there is no water to drink!" (Numbers 20:3-5)

If I were Moses, I would have answered their impertinent question, *"Why did you bring us into this wilderness?"* with my own sharp retort, *"We are in this wilderness because of your sin and unbelief – remember?"*

The Lord gave Moses clear instructions to speak to a rock and God would bring forth water. But Moses' temper (or pride) got the better of him, and instead of speaking to the rock, he struck it twice with his staff. God was not pleased with this act, and pronounced judgment upon Moses and Aaron.

> *"Because you did not trust in me enough to honor me as holy in the sight of the Israelites, you will not bring this community into the land I give them." (Numbers 20:12)*

This was hardly a storybook ending for Moses. While wandering in the wilderness over the next number of years, there were more battles with foreign powers, more revolts among the people, and no fulfilment of dreams to enter the Promised Land. You can read the record of Israel's wanderings through the wilderness in Numbers 33. All the stages of the journey are listed there – over 40 encampments.

When it was time for Moses to die, he called the people together and reminded them of the laws God had given them, their habitual faithlessness, and God's miraculous grace towards them. In Deuteronomy 32, the beautiful words of the Song of Moses are recorded. After this, Moses gives the people his last instructions:

> *"Take to heart all the words I have solemnly declared to you this day, so that you may command your children to obey carefully all the words of this law. They are not just idle words for you—they are your life. By them you will live long in the land you are crossing the Jordan to possess." (Deut. 32:46-47)*

In spite of all the trouble the people of Israel gave Moses, at the end of his life he took the time to bless the people tribe by tribe. In spite of his temper, he had a pastor's heart. He knew that his life was ultimately not about him, but about God's plan. God made His divine plan clear to him way back in Midian at the burning bush:

> *The LORD said, "I have indeed seen the misery of my people in Egypt. I have heard them crying out because of their slave drivers, and I am concerned about their suffering. So I have come down to rescue them from the hand of the Egyptians and to bring them up out of that land into a good and spacious land,*

a land flowing with milk and honey—the home of the Canaanites, Hittites, Amorites, Perizzites, Hivites and Jebusites. And now the cry of the Israelites has reached me, and I have seen the way the Egyptians are oppressing them. So now, go. I am sending you to Pharaoh to bring my people the Israelites out of Egypt."
(Ex. 3:7-10)

Ultimately, Moses was not disobedient to the directions God gave him. His life story was not about himself, but about God remembering his covenant and answering the cries of his people. Moses' life was full of unfulfilled dreams. God did not grant Moses the opportunity to enter the Promised Land. He was to die in Moab. But on Mount Nebo God showed him all of it, and reminded him:

"This is the land I promised on oath to Abraham, Isaac and Jacob when I said, 'I will give it to your descendants.' I have let you see it with your eyes, but you will not cross over into it." (Deut. 34:4)

Moses' life did not have the closure he might have sought, but it was a happy ending nonetheless.

The End of the Line

In the life of Moses, we see one of the most influential figures in the Bible, and one of the greatest leaders the world has ever known. He was the miracle worker, a friend of God, the lawgiver, the founder of theocracy, and a giant among men. What can we apply from such a life to our own?

- Moses was an imperfect human being just like us, and at first became a reluctant leader. His temper may have even been worse than mine! What made him special was that God chose him. The Lord made this clear to all his peers time and time again. We read that Moses was a very humble man; *"more humble than anyone else on the face of the earth."* (Numbers 12:3) He had greatness thrust upon him, and he rarely forgot where his power came from. When God chooses us for a task, be it ever so small or large, we are ultimately adequate for it if we walk in humble obedience with Him.

- Another lesson we can learn from Moses' life is that when God calls you to do a job, don't expect an easy, quick time of it. Only expect Him to be with you. Moses learned the meaning of hard work on the job, and had to learn to live with unfulfilled dreams.

- In the story of Moses and the Israelites of his generation, there is also a warning of the consequences of unbelief. God's path for us may seem to be wandering in a zig-zag fashion, but trying to forge straight paths for ourselves, or failing to trust Him, only makes life more of a mess. In the case of the people of Israel, it was a 40-year mess. Yet His grace stayed with His people and He faithfully brought them to the Promised Land.

- Moses never lost sight of who he was and what God had called him to do. Like another man of God many generations later – the Apostle Paul, Moses was *"not disobedient to the vision from heaven."* (Acts 26:19) In spite of his temper, he begged God to show mercy to "this stiff-necked people" on numerous occasions, when God was inclined to destroy the nation and start over. He truly was an intercessor for his people! Moses did not grow bitter the way many leaders do when the people they are leading let them down. In the end, he blessed the people, even in the midst of his own disappointment and unfulfilled dreams.

- But most of all, this is a story about the grace of God. God was working His purpose out and laying out His grand plan of redemption. Moses was caught up in God's plan. He knew there was no power in himself. God was the initiator. In our 21st Century, self-absorbed world, we do well to remember that like Moses, our lives are for His glory and not our own.

Like most of us, Moses only got to see God's winding path in retrospect, and his life was far from a simple journey. On the surface, his was a life full of "loose ends." But that was just the way the Lord wanted it for this "friend of God."

Questions for Reflection and Discussion

1. Moses forsook the luxurious life of an Egyptian prince. Why do you think he was willing to identify with the Hebrew slaves and give up "the good life?"

2. While living in the desert of Midian, Moses was surprised by the call from God in the burning bush. He became a reluctant leader – at least at first. Do you think there was a connection between Moses' reluctance and his humility? Has God ever called you to a task you were not eager to undertake? What was your response?

3. Moses' father-in-law Jethro spoke some hard truths into Moses' life, pointing out that he was trying to do everything on his own. Have you had anyone speak a difficult truth to you, and were you able to hear what they had to say?

4. Moses had a rebellion on his hands at least a dozen times. How did he deal with these persistent problems, and is there a lesson there for us?

5. Moses and the people of God had to deal with unfulfilled dreams, in part because of their own unbelief and sin. Life was full of "loose ends" for them. How might your experience be similar?

6. Moses never lost sight of the vision of the Promised Land that God gave him. His focus on God's plan sustained him. In our lives, what can sustain us in similar ways in the midst of our "wilderness" experiences?

Switchbacks

6

A Trail Back Home: RUTH AND NAOMI

"Your God will be my God." (Ruth 1:16)

The little book of Ruth nestled in the Old Testament is a jewel of Hebrew literature. It is readable, believable and touching in its compassion and love. The story of this Moabite woman is really the story of two women's lives and how God led them down a winding path to fulfillment. In truth, the book could easily be renamed the book of Naomi.

The story takes place in the time of the judges, when Israel was suffering from ups and downs in their collective walk with the Lord. It was a violent time full of disobedience, oppression, repentance and deliverance. Ruth's story is a story of light shining in a dark place. The narrative is remarkably compact; in four chapters the characters' entire lives unfold before us.

Famine and a Refugee Life

In Chapter 1, we meet the family of Elimelech from the tribe of Judah. Their home town was Bethlehem – a tiny village of no apparent significance. Elimelech had a wife Naomi and two sons, Mahlon and Kilion. The plot thickens right away when we read of a famine that had hit Israel. One does not need to read the Bible for a long time to notice there were a lot of famines taking place in the ancient world. The families of Abraham, Joseph, Elimelech, and many others all suffered because of famines. How blessed we are in America today! Famine is still a daily struggle in the lives of many throughout the world in our time. This biblical crisis was so severe that in order to survive, Elimelech took his family and moved to a foreign land – Moab – to the southeast of his own country.

And what kind of place was Moab?

It was a region southeast of the Dead Sea – due east of the region of Judah and south of the region of the tribe of Reuben. From earlier biblical history, we learn that the nation of Moab was created by the incestuous relationship Abraham's nephew Lot had with one of his daughters after the destruction of Sodom and Gomorrah. The nation that grew from this beginning was often at war with Israel and generally antagonistic toward them. At best during the time of Elimelech, the nations must have been putting up with one another during a fragile time of peace.

Few of us Americans can relate to the major upheaval this type of relocation creates. Elimelech and his family were like the many refugees of today – displaced persons seeking peace in a new land. This troubled man's plan was to live in Moab for a long time, it appears, for his two sons took Moabite wives. Such intermarriage with outsiders was not looked upon favorably by God's people. Moabites were definitely considered outsiders by Jews, and it is quite possible that the reverse was also true. Nevertheless, Elimelech and his small family sought to make new lives for themselves in a new country.

But God had other plans.

Right away in the first chapter, death struck quickly and hard. Elimelech died, and ten years later, both Mahlon and Kilion also died. All of a sudden, a story about a man's family became a story about three childless widows – Naomi, Orpah and Ruth. In the ancient world, this was the definition of destitution. Being a widow without children was a tragedy beyond all other tragedies. Naomi in particular had lost everything.

While suffering in Moab, Naomi heard the ten-year famine in Israel had subsided. She decided to return to her native town of Bethlehem. She realized that hard times awaited her there, and yet she set out with her two daughters-in-law for Israel. What a pathetic and powerless trio! Along the way, she decided to try to persuade Orpah and Ruth to leave her and return to their own people. After all, she had nothing to offer them – no new husbands from her family. She encouraged the young women to go back to their own land and find new husbands and new lives.

After many tears, Orpah left Naomi and returned to her Moabite roots. But Ruth clung to Naomi. While still on the Moabite road to Israel, Naomi continued to try to persuade Ruth to do the reasonable thing. Perhaps she said something like, *"Look at what my God has done to me. Your sister-in-law is going back to her family and her gods. You should, too. You don't want to hitch your wagon to this falling star!"*

Ruth's answer is immortalized in Scripture:

> *"Don't urge me to leave you or to turn back from you. Where you go I will go, and where you stay I will stay. Your people will be my people and your God my God. Where you die I will die, and there I will be buried. May the LORD deal with me, be it ever so severely, if even death separates you and me." (Ruth 1:16-17)*

Where did such determination and love come from? It was obviously an act of God. Why was Ruth so kind and devoted to Naomi? Her life was fastened to Naomi. What a gift of grace Ruth was to Naomi at this juncture – yet Naomi probably did not realize it. It was similar to the way in a future generation King Saul's son Jonathan's heart would be knit to David. God does something in these special relationships that is impossible to explain in earthly terms. Like the author of *Anne of Green Gables* put it, Naomi and Ruth became "kindred spirits."

But at any rate, the fragile trio that had set out from Moab had become a pitiful party of two.

When Naomi and Ruth arrived at Naomi's hometown of Bethlehem, the whole town was shocked and stirred. Naomi had been gone for over a decade, and the questions throughout Bethlehem abounded. Where was Elimelech? What had happened to their sons Mahlon and Kilion? Who was this Moabite girl, and what was she doing there? Or as it is summarized in Ruth 1:19: *"Can this be Naomi?"*

Have you ever met someone you have not seen in a while and not recognized them because of how much they have changed – usually not for the better? This is what had happened to Naomi. Imagine the gossip: *"My goodness, look at what life has done to her!"* Naomi was the talk of the town. Everyone quickly learned Naomi's sad story and about Ruth, the kind young girl living with her.

Naomi encouraged her old friends to call her by a new name:

> *"Don't call me Naomi," she told them. "Call me Mara, because the Almighty has made my life very bitter. I went away full, but the LORD has brought me back empty. Why call me Naomi? The LORD has afflicted me; the Almighty has brought misfortune upon me." (Ruth 1:20-21)*

It was not unusual in Biblical times for people to receive new names, but it may not have been common for a person to rename themselves. Naomi meant "pleasant," while Mara meant "bitter." Naomi's personal outlook on life was not a bright one. Her lament was very similar to the lament of Job. *"God has dealt harshly with me."* She really believed that her life was over. She had no male heir because of her "triple bereavement." Things appeared hopeless to her, and she had come back to die a slow, desolate death. All she had was Ruth – a single bright spot in her dark life. And Ruth's prospects were even worse than Naomi's. As a younger woman, Ruth had the long life of a poor refugee ahead of her. Her future also looked pretty dim. She was a foreigner in the land of Israel and everyone knew it. She could expect to have a hard time scratching out an existence in her new home.

But again, God had other plans for both these women.

The Barley Harvest

The only good thing that can be said about the situation at this point of the story was that the barley harvest was beginning. It was really true – the famine was over. There would be plenty of food. It was indeed a time of great celebration!

Ruth saw an opportunity to improve their lot and took initiative to help Mara (a.k.a. Naomi). She asked permission to go into the fields and gather food. Gleaning the field was hot, hard work. Ruth had not chosen an easy life. She chose to work just as a male laborer would. As she labored in the fields, she found herself on the property of a man named Boaz. He was a good, generous man, and he happened to be a relative to Naomi's late husband, Elimelech. During the day, Boaz showed up to check on how his workers were doing, and he noticed Ruth picking through the leftovers in the fields.

> *Boaz asked the overseer of his harvesters, "Who does that young woman belong to?" The overseer replied, "She is the Moabite who came back from Moab with Naomi. She said, 'Please let me glean and gather among the sheaves behind the harvesters.' She came into the field and has remained here from morning till now, except for a short rest in the shelter." (Ruth 2:5-7)*

The working men commented that Ruth had worked very hard all day – this had made an impression upon them. *"Wow, this woman works as hard as we do – perhaps even harder!"* This passage also gives more proof that everyone in town knew Naomi's sad story, and also knew about the kindness of this young Moabite widow towards her mother-in-law. Boaz did not hesitate to show exceeding kindness toward Ruth. He instructed her to only glean in his fields, where he and his men would provide her with protection. He also invited her to take rest from her labors during the day, and to enjoy food at his table along with his own servants. He gave her more grain than she possibly could have gathered on her own, and then treated her to a meal which was larger than any she had probably had in a long, long time.

Such kindness came as a complete surprise to Ruth. She asked why such generosity should be shown to a stranger and a foreigner. Boaz's response revealed much about the kind of a man he was:

> *"I've been told all about what you have done for your mother-in-law since the death of your husband—how you left your father and mother and your homeland and came to live with a people you did not know before. May the LORD repay you for what you have done. May you be richly rewarded by the LORD, the God of Israel, under whose wings you have come to take refuge." (Ruth 2:11-12)*

Boaz had a mind that saw the Lord at work in little things. He saw Ruth's kindness and rejoiced in it. He blessed her in his God's name. Yet He did not know all that God had in store for him in the story.

Mara Revived

When Ruth returned from her first day of laboring in Boaz's fields, she was carrying a surprisingly large amount of grain. Naomi (a.k.a. Mara) wanted to know who the kind benefactor was. When she discovered it was Boaz, she lit up.

> *"The LORD bless him!" Naomi said to her daughter-in-law. "He has not stopped showing his kindness to the living and the dead." She added, "That man is our close relative; he is one of our guardian-redeemers. (Ruth 2:20-21)*

In ancient Jewish culture, a guardian, or kinsman redeemer was a relative who had the obligation to watch over extended members of his family. The Old Testament law given by Moses stated that such a person should provide an heir for a brother who had died (Deut. 25:5-10); or to buy back land that a poor relative had sold outside the family (Lev. 25:25-28); or to redeem a relative who had been sold into slavery (Lev. 25:47-49). This law was common knowledge in Israel. While Ruth took the initiative to go into the fields to glean, Naomi then began to put two and two together and take initiative herself. Her hope came alive again. Her situation had "turned on a dime." God changed things in the twinkling of an eye once again, as he had for Joseph. She saw there was an opportunity for some matchmaking, and she wasted no time. Thanks to Ruth, it appeared that Naomi's new name of Mara was not going to stick after all.

In Chapter 3, Naomi began to unfold her plan. She instructed Ruth to put on her best clothes and perfume – in other words, to adorn herself like a bride – and sneak down to the threshing floor where Boaz had been working, and lie at his feet after he had fallen asleep. Naomi knew that Ruth would eventually be discovered there by Boaz, and he would get the message loud and clear.

But Ruth would be risking her reputation by acting in such a manner. What if she were seen by the working men? Wouldn't people have thought she was a prostitute? Why should she care about this Jewish family line? In spite of these risks and questions, she made herself completely vulnerable to Boaz by uncovering his feet and sleeping on the threshing floor among all the working men. A startled Boaz woke in the night to discover this young woman at his feet and wondered what was going on.

> *In the middle of the night something startled the man; he turned—and there was a woman lying at his feet! "Who are you?" he asked.*
>
> *"I am your servant Ruth," she said. "Spread the corner of your garment over me, since you are a guardian-redeemer of our family."*
>
> *"The LORD bless you, my daughter," he replied. "This kindness is greater than that which you showed earlier: You have not run after the younger men, whether rich or poor. And now, my daughter, don't be afraid. I will do for you all you ask. All the people of my town know that you are a woman of noble character. Although it is true that I am a guardian-redeemer of our family, there is another who is more closely related than I. Stay here for the night, and in the morning if he wants to do his duty as your guardian-redeemer, good; let him redeem you. But if he is not willing, as surely as the LORD lives I will do it. Lie here until morning." (Ruth 3:8-13)*

This is one of the only times in Scripture that a marriage proposal is made by a woman to a man! Naomi knew that Boaz knew the laws concerning the kinsman redeemer, and all would be well.

Joy Out of Sorrow

The rest of the story really is a filmmaker's dream. Sure enough, Naomi's matchmaking worked like a charm. Boaz realized his moral and legal obligation and wasted no time seeing that justice was done for Naomi and Ruth. To his credit, he acted immediately to bring justice to Naomi and the family of Elimelech. He eventually married Ruth, continued Elimelech's family line, and this union brought a son into the world. This child in essence became Naomi's son, and once again, this news became the talk of the town:

> *The women said to Naomi: "Praise be to the LORD, who this day has not left you without a guardian-redeemer. May [this baby boy] become famous*

throughout Israel! He will renew your life and sustain you in your old age. For your daughter-in-law, who loves you and who is better to you than seven sons, has given him birth." Then Naomi took the child in her arms and cared for him. The women living there said, "Naomi has a son!" And they named him Obed. He was the father of Jesse, the father of David. (Ruth 4:14-17)

This is a story of two people acting graciously and doing the kind and righteous thing. Both Ruth and Boaz were redeemers in Naomi's life. And even though Naomi tried to rename herself, her original name remained intact.

The End of the Line

What do we learn from this beautiful story?

- Ruth's life's path is tied to the path of Naomi, which has many crooked turns. Life throws painful events at us frequently – many times involving the death of those we love. Remember one of Jacob's scars – Rachel's death. Remarkably, all the pain that Naomi experienced, Ruth chose to take on as her own. As Boaz stated, Ruth chose to seek refuge under the God of Israel's wings (Ruth 2:12), and the Lord blessed her for it. We can take refuge under these same wings.

- Ruth is one of the few characters in the Bible where nothing negative is said about her, other than that she was a Moabitess. In contrast to the choices other biblical figures made in their lives, including Abraham and Jacob, her choices avoided more painful detours in her journey. Her positive choices led to positive results, but they involved risk and hard work. She chose wisely, and by God's grace, so can we.

- Ruth became a redeeming force in her mother-in-law's life, and changed the history of the world in the process. She was the great grandmother of King David! Her selfless acts of mercy are a tribute to her character and a stellar example for us. Who can tell what God will bring forth from our acts of mercy and obedience?

- After Naomi had given up hope, she came to realize that there are good people in the world after all. God does not leave Himself without a witness, and he provided "redeemers" for Naomi in Ruth and Boaz. Quite often, He will graciously provide people in our lives as well, and perhaps we can be agents of redemption for others, too.

The loving and gracious acts of Ruth and Boaz are a foreshadowing of the work of the Great Redeemer, Jesus Christ. These words penned by Keith Green are true:

> *There is a Redeemer, Jesus God's own Son, Precious Lamb of God, Messiah, Holy One. Thank you, O my Father, For giving us your Son, And leaving your Spirit till the work on earth is done.*

Questions for Reflection and Discussion

1. This story begins with a series of deaths of several family members. Sadly, death is a part of all our lives. Talk about the pain of grief and how people often react to the death of loved ones.

2. Ruth's devotion to Naomi defies logical explanation. At the very least, it is surprisingly strong. Why do you think they became such "kindred spirits?" Have you ever experienced a similar friendship with someone of a different generation? How can you explain such relationships?

3. When Naomi returned to her hometown, she changed her name to "Mara," which means "bitter." Perhaps this was a result of her giving up all hope. Have you ever been tempted to act in a similar manner? What does hopelessness do to a person?

4. Reflect on how quickly God broke into Naomi's situation and note how He used godly people to change the situation. What lessons are in this sudden change that might apply to us?

Switchbacks

7

The Long Road to a Crown: DAVID

"But David found strength in the LORD his God." (I Samuel 30:6)

As we saw with Abraham, the pathway to a promise can be a long and winding trail and an uphill journey full of switchbacks. It was for David.

Background

Almost 500 years had passed by between Moses and David's time. The people of Israel had entered and conquered the Promised Land by the hand of God. There had been times of faithfulness and times of falling away under the period of the Judges, when God would raise up leaders to deliver his people from foreign oppression brought on by their sin and folly. Eventually the people clamored for a king, so that they could be like the other nations. The last judge, Samuel, reluctantly consented to their request and Saul was anointed king over all Israel.

But Saul proved himself to be unequal to the task. His heart was not right before God, and the Lord tore the kingdom from his hands. God did not accomplish this overnight, but his purposes could not be thwarted. God had chosen another man to shepherd his people.

David enters the narrative in I Samuel 16. Samuel was grieving over having anointed Saul king, but the Lord told him to get over it and move on.

> *The LORD said to Samuel, "How long will you mourn for Saul, since I have rejected him as king over Israel? Fill your horn with oil and be on your way; I am sending you to Jesse of Bethlehem. I have chosen one of his sons to be king." (I Samuel 16:1)*

Perhaps God has spoken to you the way he did to Samuel: *"Stop pouting – I have work for you to do."* There are times when we have to "fill our horn with oil" and be on our way. God was moving on, and so Samuel traveled to the house of Jesse in Bethlehem.

You may remember Bethlehem was the tiny town Naomi was from. Jesse, the grandson of Ruth and Boaz, was a man with eight sons. A banquet was held in Samuel's honor, and Samuel eagerly awaited for the Lord to reveal to him which son was to be Israel's next king. Samuel saw the eldest son Eliab and jumped to conclusions.

> *When they arrived, Samuel saw Eliab and thought, "Surely the LORD's anointed stands here before the LORD." But the LORD said to Samuel, "Do not consider his appearance or his height, for I have rejected him. The LORD does not look at the things people look at. People look at the outward appearance, but the LORD looks at the heart." (I Samuel 16:6-7)*

The first seven of Jesse's sons passed before Samuel, but the Lord let him know that God had not chosen any of them. Son number eight was missing – the runt of the litter had not even been invited to the banquet! Samuel asked Jesse a final question:

> *"Are these all the sons you have?" "There is still the youngest," Jesse answered. "He is tending the sheep." Samuel said, "Send for him; we will not sit down until he arrives." So he sent for him and had him brought in. He was glowing with health and had a fine appearance and handsome features. Then the LORD said, "Rise and anoint him; this is the one." So Samuel took the horn of oil and anointed him in the presence of his brothers, and from that day on the Spirit of the LORD came powerfully upon David. (I Samuel 16:11-13)*

I cannot help but wonder what this public ceremony did to the family dynamics and sibling rivalry. I am sure Samuel's choice confounded all of Jesse's clan. David was the least in the family, and yet God chose him because of his heart. And not only had God chosen David, but His Spirit was now powerfully upon him.

Contrasting to this, we read the Spirit of the Lord had departed from King Saul, and he was plagued by an evil spirit. His attendants recommended some music therapy, and one of his servants knew of a fine harp player – David, a son of Jesse. David was summoned to play for the king when he was tormented, and his playing eased Saul's pain.

David was described even at this early stage of the story in glowing terms:

> *"I have seen a son of Jesse of Bethlehem who knows how to play the lyre. He is a brave man and a warrior. He speaks well and is a fine-looking man. And the LORD is with him." (I Samuel 16:18)*

So, the young David entered Saul's service – at least part-time. This was a time in David's life where he was holding down multiple jobs. He was still a shepherd for his father, a music therapist/court musician, an armor bearer for Saul, and an errand runner for Jesse to the front. To use a modern term, David was multitasking. (I Sam.17:15)

Goliath

In the midst of this busy schedule, David reached one of the major turning points in his young life. If you want to get a job done, give it to a busy person!

David was sent on an errand by his father Jesse to take some food to his older brothers in Saul's army, and to bring back news from the battlefront. When he arrived to see his brothers, he found the armies of Israel lined up for battle in the Valley of Elah against their perennial enemy, the Philistines. The Philistines had a champion – a nine-foot-tall giant named Goliath. For days he had stood out in front of Saul's troops and challenged them to produce one man to fight him in a winner-take-all contest.

Israel's army was dismayed and terrified. Like the spies returning from Canaan hundreds of years earlier in Moses' day, the Jews felt like grasshoppers before Goliath. Saul had offered a huge reward to any man who would face Goliath: complete tax exemption for his family, lots of cash and even his daughter. But no one had stepped forward. At least, no one until the day David arrived.

> *When David arrived at the front, he greeted his brothers. As he was talking with them, Goliath, the Philistine champion from Gath, stepped out from his lines and shouted his usual defiance, and David heard it. (I Samuel 17:23)*

The longstanding problem of the Philistine giant might have gone on indefinitely. It was a military stalemate. But as He had in the past, God was about to work a sudden solution to a prolonged problem. The difference this day from other days was that David heard the taunts of the giant. He was a young man on whom the Spirit of God had rested with power. His reaction was completely different from everyone else's. His blood started to boil. He started to dig for more information about this situation.

> *David asked the men standing near him, "What will be done for the man who kills this Philistine and removes this disgrace from Israel? Who is this uncircumcised Philistine that he should defy the armies of the living God?" (I Samuel 17:26)*

David's words reveal much about him at this point in his life. He was zealous for the Lord, and saw Goliath's presence as a disgrace and an affront to his God. He was filled with righteous indignation. Like Caleb and Joshua generations earlier, he believed that God could deliver his people when facing giants. David's response was not to look at his own shortcomings (literally) in the light of Goliath, but to look at Goliath's shortcomings in the light of Israel's God.

There are those among the armies of Israel who were skeptical of David's intentions. His oldest brother Eliab rebuked David, viewing him with suspicion and anger. In short, he said something like, *"You cocky little runt! You are so conceited and wicked! You just came down here to watch the battle in hopes of seeing some bloodshed. You think the gore of war is just a fun time!"* (I Samuel 17:28)

Eliab completely missed the moving of the Spirit of God in David. Remember, Eliab had seen his baby brother anointed by Samuel, while he had been passed over. Perhaps he could not get over his own jealousy. But in spite of brotherly opposition, David was brought to Saul.

David said to Saul, *"Let no one lose heart on account of this Philistine; your servant will go and fight him."* (I Samuel 17:32)

Because David was so young, King Saul was extremely skeptical. Humanly speaking, the warrior king knew there was no way a boy could beat a nine-foot tall Philistine.

But David insisted he could do it.

> *"Your servant has been keeping his father's sheep. When a lion or a bear came and carried off a sheep from the flock, I went after it, struck it and rescued the sheep from its mouth. When it turned on me, I seized it by its hair, struck it and killed it. Your servant has killed both the lion and the bear; this uncircumcised Philistine will be like one of them, because he has defied the armies of the living God. The LORD who rescued me from the paw of the lion and the paw of the bear will rescue me from the hand of this Philistine."* (I Samuel 17:34-37)

So, Saul relented and the lopsided contest was on.

We all know the outcome. It is one of the most retold stories in the Bible. The young David fought in the name of the Lord with a staff, his shepherd's bag, a handful of smooth stones and a sling. He put his young life on the line as a witness for the Lord for all the world to see. He killed Goliath with a stone and a sling. Notice how David talked to Goliath when they came face to face:

> *"You come against me with sword and spear and javelin, but I come against you in the name of the LORD Almighty, the God of the armies of Israel, whom you have defied. This day the LORD will deliver you into my hands, and I'll strike*

you down and cut off your head. This very day I will give the carcasses of the Philistine army to the birds and the wild animals, and the whole world will know that there is a God in Israel. All those gathered here will know that it is not by sword or spear that the LORD saves; for the battle is the LORD's, and he will give all of you into our hands." (I Samuel 17:45-47)

In the sports world, David's statements would be referred to as "trash talk." The Spirit of the Lord was truly upon this young man. He had become a prophet warrior! As these events were unfolding, Saul's commander Abner did not know who David was, and Saul did not remember him either. David was still a nobody in their eyes.

Through an act of great faith and bravery, David's life changed. He was to be with Saul full-time from then on.

Life with Saul

If we were to expect some "straight paths" to appear in David's life, this would be the point in time for them. David had won a great victory for Israel, and one might expect him to ascend through the ranks and eventually experience universal acclaim as hero and king. This was not exactly what God had in mind.

After the victory over Goliath and the Philistines, at least two significant things happened in David's life. They revolved around Jonathan, King Saul's son and heir, and the King himself.

First, we read in I Samuel 18 that after Goliath was slain, Jonathan was inspired to become David's close friend.

After David had finished talking with Saul, Jonathan became one in spirit with David, and he loved him as himself. From that day Saul kept David with him and did not let him return home to his family. And Jonathan made a covenant with David because he loved him as himself. Jonathan took off the robe he was wearing and gave it to David, along with his tunic, and even his sword, his bow and his belt. (I Samuel 18:1-4)

This act of God's grace through a person is similar to what happened to Naomi through Ruth, her daughter-in-law. It was an unexplainable attachment. Jonathan saw that God was with David, and he rejoiced in it. He wanted to be a part of what God was doing. Jonathan became the close, loyal brother that David had not yet had in his life.

In contrast to the disdain and contempt he received at the hand of his eldest brother Eliab, David received from Jonathan unconditional love and loyalty.

Secondly, and in stark contrast to this, Saul's admiration of David quickly turned to jealousy and suspicion. It is interesting how the same actions by David – military victories won by great faith – brought out such different reactions in the hearts of others.

> *When the men were returning home after David had killed the Philistine, the women came out from all the towns of Israel to meet King Saul with singing and dancing, with joyful songs and with timbrels and lyres. As they danced, they sang:*
>
> *"Saul has slain his thousands, and David his tens of thousands." Saul was very angry; this refrain displeased him greatly. "They have credited David with tens of thousands," he thought, "but me with only thousands. What more can he get but the kingdom?" And from that time on Saul kept a close eye on David.*
> *(I Samuel 18:6-9)*

During David's early years of soldiering for Saul, we see him as a faithful officer and a humble servant to his king. He won great victories, but turned down opportunities for preferential treatment and personal advancement. He was even offered the hand of King Saul's oldest daughter Merab, but he turned down the honor. *"Who am I, and what is my family or my clan in Israel, that I should become the king's son-in-law?"* (I Sam. 18:18) Later he was offered the hand of another daughter, Michal. His initial reaction to the opportunity showed the same humility: *"Do you think it is a small matter to become the king's son-in-law? I'm only a poor man and little known."* (I Samuel 18:23)

Saul began to fear David, because he knew the Lord was with David and God's presence was sorely lacking in his own life. His fear and jealousy escalated over time. He sent David into dangerous battles hoping he would be killed. Later, while experiencing one of his dark, brooding moods, he hurled a spear at David, attempting to pin him to the wall. Then he sent soldiers to David's house to kill him in his sleep. Through all of these trials, Jonathan held on to the belief that Saul was not really out to kill David. Jonathan believed the best of both his father and his friend. But over time, even Jonathan became disgusted by his father's vendetta against David, because it was utterly baseless. King Saul's fears rose to the point of complete paranoia, and in the end, this could not be hidden from anyone. For no reason but jealousy, David became Public Enemy Number One, and everyone wishing to get on the good side of King Saul became a threat to David's life. His fugitive years were about to begin.

Life on the Run

David was driven from everything that brought him comfort and joy – his land, his people, his king, and his security. Everything except his God. And yet, he was walking in the center of God's will for his life. When David began to run, he fled to Samuel, the man of God who anointed him years earlier, and told him of how he had been mistreated. David's friends at this point in his life were few and far between.

David was a victim of hatred and jealousy at the hands of the most powerful man in Israel. Miraculously, David eluded Saul time and time again. For years, David was the most hunted man in the nation. Those who helped David did so at the risk of their lives, including Jonathan (who had a spear thrown at him by his own father) and the priests in Ahimelech's clan (whom Saul executed).

David even had to flee to the land of the Philistines and feign insanity in order to survive. What kept him going? We gain insight from one of David's psalms written in the midst of his troubles:

> *I will extol the LORD at all times; his praise will always be on my lips. I will glory in the LORD; let the afflicted hear and rejoice. Glorify the LORD with me; let us exalt his name together.*
>
> *I sought the LORD, and he answered me; he delivered me from all my fears. Those who look to him are radiant; their faces are never covered with shame. This poor man called, and the LORD heard him; he saved him out of all his troubles. The angel of the LORD encamps around those who fear him, and he delivers them.*
>
> *Taste and see that the LORD is good; blessed is the one who takes refuge in him. (Psalm 34:1-8)*

We get a glimpse of David's coping strategy in life. It involved music, poetry, worship and praising God. David knew he was walking with God and was blameless, and that God would honor him.

During his years as a fugitive, David hid in caves, in forests, in deserts, and in foreign lands. It was far from a pleasant life. His brothers eventually came to support him, along with a band of about 400 disenfranchised men. He was on the run constantly. In I Samuel 23, David heard of a small Hebrew town called Keilah being in peril from Philistine assault. He inquired of the Lord before going to their rescue. The Lord gave him assurance of success, but such action was full of peril. Not only might the Philistines defeat his small band of fighters, but Saul may hear of his whereabouts and come to kill him. In spite of these dangers, David fought the Philistines and saved the town of Keilah.

But shortly thereafter, Saul mustered his army and headed for the area. Sure enough, he had been informed of David's location. David inquired of the Lord and learned that the people of the town would hand David over in spite of his recent efforts on their behalf. So, he had to leave the security of the town and head for the hills once again. That was the thanks he got for saving them!

In seemed that everywhere David went, informants betrayed him to Saul. If any man had a right to be paranoid, it would be David. It is not paranoia if people really are after you.

Soon after the Keilah incident, David had chances to kill Saul and end the injustice. In the Desert of En Gedi, Saul entered a cave where David was hiding. Lucky circumstances handed Saul to David on a silver platter. His men urged him to slay Saul, but he refused:

> *"The LORD forbid that I should do such a thing to my master, the LORD's anointed, or lay my hand on him; for he is the anointed of the LORD." With these words David sharply rebuked his men and did not allow them to attack Saul. And Saul left the cave and went his way. (I Samuel 24:6-7)*

David passed up the chance to create his own straighter path by letting the wicked king live. Saul was the Lord's anointed. God would vindicate David in his good time. He was willing to wait and not run ahead of God. David did not take justice into his own hands in this situation. But he came very close to doing it in another situation which did not involve Saul.

Nabal and Abigail

In I Samuel 25, we read of an event in David's life where he faced a major temptation to be judge, jury and executioner in the face of injustice. Thanks to a brave and wise woman, David avoided committing a great sin.

While David would put up with abuse from Saul, it appeared he would not always put up with it from others who wronged him. David and his band of men assisted and protected many fellow Jews who were in need around him. One such man was Nabal, a rich shepherd. David camped near his herds and made sure they were protected, and that Nabal's servants did not lose anything of their master's. As a former shepherd, David knew how valuable a service he was providing to Nabal. At the festive sheep shearing time, David asked for kindness and a bit of remuneration, but Nabal snubbed him big time:

> *"Who is this David? Who is this son of Jesse? Many servants are breaking away from their masters these days. Why should I take my bread and water, and the meat I have slaughtered for my shearers, and give it to men coming from who knows where?" (I Samuel 25:10-11)*

Nabal had to know who David was – everyone in Israel knew the story of the son of Jesse. This ungrateful man was intentionally insulting David out of greed and selfishness. Upon hearing Nabal's terse reply, David completely flew off the handle. This affront was apparently more than he could bear. David ordered his men to put on their swords and prepare for battle against Nabal. His plan was to annihilate Nabal's house and take all his possessions as his rightful reward. He was ready to avenge himself, and his proposed punishment did not fit Nabal's crime. Quite literally, it would have been overkill.

> *"It's been useless—all my watching over this fellow's property in the wilderness so that nothing of his was missing. He has paid me back evil for good. May God deal with David, be it ever so severely, if by morning I leave alive one male of all who belong to him!" (I Samuel 25:21-22)*

David was bitter and primed for bloody revenge. He seemed more than ready to rush along his own straight path and resolve this injustice.

Some unnamed servants in Nabal's household informed their master's wife of the insult. At that point, only one person stood in the way of an impending bloodbath. Nabal's wife Abigail learned of her foolish husband's rebuff of David's kindness and immediately took matters into her own hands. She gathered a relatively small supply of food and gifts for David and his men and hurriedly set out to intercept him. She courageously spoke to David and placated him.

> *When Abigail saw David, she quickly got off her donkey and bowed down before David with her face to the ground. She fell at his feet and said: "Pardon your servant, my lord, and let me speak to you; hear what your servant has to say. Please pay no attention, my lord, to that wicked man Nabal. He is just like his name—his name means Fool, and folly goes with him. And as for me, your servant, I did not see the men my lord sent. And now, my lord, as surely as the Lord your God lives and as you live, since the Lord has kept you from bloodshed and from avenging yourself with your own hands, may your enemies and all who*

> *are intent on harming my lord be like Nabal. And let this gift, which your servant has brought to my lord, be given to the men who follow you.*
>
> *"Please forgive your servant's presumption. The Lord your God will certainly make a lasting dynasty for my lord, because you fight the Lord's battles, and no wrongdoing will be found in you as long as you live. Even though someone is pursuing you to take your life, the life of my lord will be bound securely in the bundle of the living by the LORD your God, but the lives of your enemies he will hurl away as from the pocket of a sling. When the LORD has fulfilled for my lord every good thing he promised concerning him and has appointed him ruler over Israel, my lord will not have on his conscience the staggering burden of needless bloodshed or of having avenged himself. And when the LORD your God has brought my lord success, remember your servant." (I Samuel 25:23-31)*

Abigail was a remarkable woman – quick-thinking, resourceful, and courageous. Abigail's message to David was: *"You fight the Lord's battles, let Him fight yours."* Much to his credit, David immediately saw the hand of God in this encounter.

> *David said to Abigail, "Praise be to the LORD, the God of Israel, who has sent you today to meet me. May you be blessed for your good judgment and for keeping me from bloodshed this day and from avenging myself with my own hands. Otherwise, as surely as the LORD, the God of Israel, lives, who has kept me from harming you, if you had not come quickly to meet me, not one male belonging to Nabal would have been left alive by daybreak." Then David accepted from her hand what she had brought him and said, "Go home in peace. I have heard your words and granted your request." (I Samuel 25:32-35)*

Nabal's insult of David was almost the straw that broke the camel's back – but for the grace of God, the quick actions of some unknown servants in Nabal's house, and the wisdom of Abigail. By the end of the story, Nabal had died and David took the widow Abigail to be his wife.

Abigail's words must have rung in David's ears for years to come. *"Fight the Lord's battles, and let him fight yours!"* His life was often marked by refusing to take vengeance upon those who wronged him.

Settling in Philistia

David had a second chance to kill the wicked King Saul. The King of Israel had been tipped off as to David's whereabouts and came after him again in the Desert of Ziph. David and his captain Abishai snuck into Saul's camp at night. They were able to do this because the Lord had put Saul and his men into a deep sleep. The two intruders crept up to Saul. Abishai wished to pin Saul to the ground with his spear and end all this running, hiding and injustice, but David stopped him.

> *Abishai said to David, "Today God has delivered your enemy into your hands. Now let me pin him to the ground with one thrust of the spear; I won't strike him twice."*
>
> *But David said to Abishai, "Don't destroy him! Who can lay a hand on the LORD's anointed and be guiltless? As surely as the LORD lives," he said, "the LORD himself will strike him, or his time will come and he will die, or he will go into battle and perish. But the LORD forbid that I should lay a hand on the LORD's anointed." (I Samuel 26:8-11)*

Instead they simply took Saul's spear and water jug to prove they had been there, and called out to Saul. David stated his case before Saul and his armies, declaring his innocence.

> *"Why is my lord pursuing his servant? What have I done, and what wrong am I guilty of? Now let my lord the king listen to his servant's words. If the LORD has incited you against me, then may he accept an offering. If, however, people have done it, may they be cursed before the LORD! They have driven me today from my share in the LORD's inheritance and have said, 'Go, serve other gods.' Now do not let my blood fall to the ground far from the presence of the LORD. The king of Israel has come out to look for a flea—as one hunts a partridge in the mountains." (I Samuel 26:18-20)*

Saul had another brief change of heart and broke off his manhunt. But David knew this peace was only temporary. He believed that living as a fugitive within the boundaries of Israel would eventually lead to his capture and death. He decided to take refuge in the land of the Philistines, where Saul could not reach him.

David and his band, now numbering 600 men, joined forces with the Philistine King Achish. David was given his own town of Ziklag, and he lived there for a total of 16 months. During this time, he appeared to be a faithful subject to Achish, and the pagan king viewed him as a reliable military asset. But when it came time for Achish to go to war against Saul and the armies of Israel, the other Philistine generals refused to bring David and his men along, for fear they would turn on them during the battle. On the eve of the battle, King Achish sent David back to his town of Ziklag.

Unbeknownst to them, while David and his men had been away preparing for war, a tragedy had suddenly struck them. The Amalekites had raided and burned their new home town of Ziklag and taken all the women and possessions as booty. David and his men were then in a foreign land and had lost everything.

We read in I Samuel 30 that David and his men wept aloud until they had no strength left to weep. The men's sorrow and grief were so great, they even talked of stoning David to death.

Pause and look at David's life at this juncture. He was perhaps at his absolute lowest point. He had been anointed as a boy to become king, and by faith he knew that God would eventually bring him to the throne. He had been a faithful champion for Israel and yet he was being pursued by a jealous, wicked king. He was a victim of a great injustice, and was a stranger in a strange land. On top of this, he had lost everything in an Amalekite raid and was about to be killed by the only friends he had left on the face of the earth. Why had God allowed all this happen? If I were David, I would be praying for God to let me travel some straight, easy paths for a change. At the very least, I would be questioning what God was doing.

What did David do next?

"But David found strength in the LORD his God." (I Samuel 30:6)

What a great verse! Instead of turning away from God during this crisis, David ran into the arms of God for strength and consolation, and then he began to take action. In life, sometimes God's people face terrible injustice and persecution. God may allow evil to dominate for a time to test and refine us. Trials come – what do we make of them? What did David make of them?

David found strength in the LORD his God. Wicked men were easy to find – even among his own men. But David was different. He was indeed a man after God's own heart.

David followed his habitual pattern – once again, he inquired of the Lord: *"Shall I pursue this raiding party? Will I overtake them?"* (I Samuel 30:8) The Lord answered in the affirmative. He obeyed and recovered all that was taken. Meanwhile, during this time of personal crisis for David and his men, God had been working His purpose out on Mount Gilboa.

Saul's End and David's Beginning

Saul and Jonathan both died in the ensuing battle against the Philistines – the one in which David was forbidden to participate by King Achish. The book of I Samuel ends with the death and burial of King Saul and his sons. After David's victory over the raiding Amalekites and his return to Ziklag, he received word of the death of Saul and Jonathan. He mourned for their loss, and stayed in Ziklag for a time. Eventually, David inquired of the Lord again as to whether or not he should return to Judah, and the Lord directed him to do so.

David had seen God avenge his shameful and unjust treatment at the hands of King Saul. He knew God would place him on the throne of all Israel and fulfill His promises. Perhaps David was expecting a quick resolution to all his problems now that Saul was gone. But it would take another seven and a half years before his dreams and God's plan came to fruition. David was indeed walking a long and winding path – one that was uphill a lot of the time!

Upon his arrival back in his homeland with his 600 men and all their families, he was anointed King of Judah – but not over all of Israel. To his credit, David did not seem to be in a hurry to grab the throne. He continued to wait upon God and His timing.

While Judah had rallied around David, the rest of Israel had anointed Saul's 40-year-old surviving son, Ish-Bosheth. This was largely due to the work and influence of Saul's great general, Abner. Inevitably, civil war broke out. David would not become king over all Israel without a fight. Eventually, God's plan was accomplished. Along the way there was plenty of political intrigue, deception and even murder on the part of David's general Joab, who took justice into his own hands. Abner was murdered by Joab. Ish-Bosheth was assassinated by the brothers Recab and Baanah. To David's credit, he condemned such actions. In his mind, the ends did not justify the means.

King David

After seven years of being king over the tribe of Judah, God's purpose for David is finally accomplished.

All the tribes of Israel came to David at Hebron and said,

David Rox

"We are your own flesh and blood. In the past, while Saul was king over us, you were the one who led Israel on their military campaigns. And the Lord said to you, 'You will shepherd my people Israel, and you will become their ruler.'" When all the elders of Israel had come to King David at Hebron, the king made a covenant with them at Hebron before the LORD, and they anointed David king over Israel. (II Samuel 5:1-3)

When David was finally anointed king over all Israel, he continued to fight the Lord's battles. He entered into a series of military ventures against the Philistines and other nations, and God gave him victory after victory. He was truly the warrior king. He was God's man, and the people knew it and came to love him.

He conquered the city of Jerusalem and it became known as his capital. He then brought the ark of the Covenant into Jerusalem with great celebration. Along the way, he built a great palace for himself. God gave David and the land a time of peace from all their enemies.

David turned his heart towards building a temple for the Lord in Jerusalem, but God made it known to him that this task would pass on to his son. While David wanted to do something special for the Lord, God made promises beyond anything David could have imagined. The Lord sent a message to King David through the prophet Nathan.

"The LORD declares to you that the LORD himself will establish a house for you: When your days are over and you rest with your ancestors, I will raise up your offspring to succeed you, your own flesh and blood, and I will establish his kingdom. He is the one who will build a house for my Name, and I will establish the throne of his kingdom forever. I will be his father, and he will be my son. When he does wrong, I will punish him with a rod wielded by men, with floggings inflicted by human hands. But my love will never be taken away from him, as I took it away from Saul, whom I removed from before you. Your house and your kingdom will endure forever before me; your throne will be established forever.'" (II Samuel 7:11-16)

Instead of building a house for God, God promised to build an eternal dynasty for David and his descendants. David came to realize he could not out-give God. David's response was to offer a great prayer of praise and thanksgiving to the Lord.

Then King David went in and sat before the LORD, and he said: "Who am I, Sovereign LORD, and what is my family, that you have brought me this far?

And as if this were not enough in your sight, Sovereign LORD, you have also spoken about the future of the house of your servant—and this decree, Sovereign LORD, is for a mere human!

"What more can David say to you? For you know your servant, Sovereign LORD. For the sake of your word and according to your will, you have done this great thing and made it known to your servant.

"How great you are, Sovereign LORD! There is no one like you, and there is no God but you, as we have heard with our own ears. And who is like your people Israel—the one nation on earth that God went out to redeem as a people for himself, and to make a name for himself, and to perform great and awesome wonders by driving out nations and their gods from before your people, whom you redeemed from Egypt? You have established your people Israel as your very own forever, and you, LORD, have become their God.

"And now, LORD God, keep forever the promise you have made concerning your servant and his house. Do as you promised, so that your name will be great forever. Then people will say, 'The LORD Almighty is God over Israel!' And the house of your servant David will be established in your sight.

"LORD Almighty, God of Israel, you have revealed this to your servant, saying, 'I will build a house for you.' So your servant has found courage to pray this prayer to you. Sovereign LORD, you are God! Your covenant is trustworthy, and you have promised these good things to your servant. Now be pleased to bless the house of your servant, that it may continue forever in your sight; for you, Sovereign LORD, have spoken, and with your blessing the house of your servant will be blessed forever." (II Samuel 7:18-29)

David talked to God like a close friend. All of David's life was lived before God, and he invited Him into every nook and cranny of it. For a time, King David and his nation enjoyed a time of peace and great prosperity. It seemed that God finally wanted to open some straight trails for David and his nation to travel. If they could walk in obedience, his blessings would not depart from them. Sadly, human nature got in the way. God had chosen David, and the king had not forgotten it up to this point. But he was about to on one spring evening.

Bathsheba and the Consequences

One fateful spring, instead of going out to war with his men, David stayed in his comfortable palace and saw a woman bathing on a rooftop. With the woman Bathsheba, the wife of one of his captains, David fell into lust, fornication, adultery, an illegitimate pregnancy, deception, and eventually murder. His actions in killing Bathsheba's husband Uriah the Hittite were similar to the actions of King Saul, when he tried to get David killed in battle. That is how low David had sunk in his character! He had created his own wicked road to satisfy his lust and personal agenda.

How could this have happened? Did David get tired? Lazy? Complacent? Conceited? Probably some combination of all of these vices. The consequences were more than tragic for David, his family, and his nation.

After Uriah the Hittite was conveniently dead, David thought he had gotten away with his cover up. He had another lovely wife and another child on the way. However, we read in II Samuel 11:27, *"But the thing that David had done displeased the LORD."* God sent the prophet Nathan to David and made it known that God had seen it all.

> *Then Nathan said to David, "You are the man! This is what the LORD, the God of Israel, says: 'I anointed you king over Israel, and I delivered you from the hand of Saul. I gave your master's house to you, and your master's wives into your arms. I gave you all Israel and Judah. And if all this had been too little, I would have given you even more. Why did you despise the word of the LORD by doing what is evil in his eyes? You struck down Uriah the Hittite with the sword and took his wife to be your own. You killed him with the sword of the Ammonites. Now, therefore, the sword will never depart from your house, because you despised me and took the wife of Uriah the Hittite to be your own.'*
>
> *"This is what the LORD says: 'Out of your own household I am going to bring calamity on you. Before your very eyes I will take your wives and give them to one who is close to you, and he will sleep with your wives in broad daylight. You did it in secret, but I will do this thing in broad daylight before all Israel.'"* (II Samuel 12:7-12)

David's heart was turned back to the Lord and he truly repented of his great sin. But there were still consequences for him and all Israel. Bathsheba's newborn son was to die. And even worse than this, the sword did not depart from David's family. In the years that followed, one of David's sons raped his half-sister (Amnon and Tamar); another son murdered his half-brother (Amnon and Absalom), and another son Absalom was killed while leading a rebellion trying to overthrow King David himself. The blessings promised by God were disrupted by the sin of one godly man. God was poised to bestow upon David even more blessings than He had, but his own sin robbed him. How tragic!

We can easily see how bad David's sin was, but we should also see how great God's grace was to David to forgive his sin. And likewise, we need to see how bad our sins are and how great the grace is for God to forgive us!

Even in the midst of these events, God's sovereign plan won the day.

The Latter Days of the King

The rebellion of David's son Absalom was a near death experience for David, but he was restored as king after seeing his son murdered by Joab, the head of David's army. We might think that after this harrowing experience, David would enjoy peace in his old age. But his troubles were not over.

Due to jealousy and strife between the clans of Israel, a troublemaker from the tribe of Benjamin named Sheba led an unsuccessful rebellion. Perhaps it is no coincidence that Sheba was from the same tribe (Benjamin) as the former King Saul. A major insurrection followed, and David had to flee for his life for a time. We read about this trouble in II Samuel 20. It seemed that David's throne was in constant jeopardy. The earlier days of being a fugitive never completely went away.

One of the final royal acts of David was another blot on his record. He decided to number his armies and took a census – even against the advice of his generals. David failed to seek the Lord on this point, contrary to what he had done so many times earlier in his life. For a short time, David seemed to seek security in numbers rather than in his God. How far away this was from his battle with Goliath! There is a biblical principle at work in this story: just because a person is righteous today does not insure he will be righteous tomorrow. Our old sinful natures have a way of coming to the surface when we least expect it.

David learned from the census that he had an army of well over a million men, but this act displeased the Lord. To David's credit, he quickly realized after counting his fighting men that he had sinned.

> *David was conscience-stricken after he had counted the fighting men, and he said to the LORD, "I have sinned greatly in what I have done. Now, LORD, I*

beg you, take away the guilt of your servant. I have done a very foolish thing."
(II Samuel 24:10)

The Lord sent another prophet to David. Gad delivered a message of judgment to the king. David was to choose between three odious options: three years of famine, three months of fleeing from his enemies, or three days of plague. A three-year long famine would be disastrous, and David had suffered enough from running from his enemies. So, he chose the shortest option, and 70,000 of his subjects throughout Israel died. It is said the only mistakes leaders make are big ones; this was certainly the case with David and the census.

David was an old man, and there was a clamoring for his throne. The national question became, "who will be David's successor?" Another one of David's sons, Adonijah, put himself forward as king. Even David's chief general Joab and the priest Abiathar supported Adonijah's claim to the throne, and this strong alliance presented a threat to David's real choice for his successor – Bathsheba's son Solomon. David anointed Solomon, but the political wrangling and intrigue continued even after David's death.

As David's life drew to its conclusion, there were still a lot of loose ends. There was no "all-sunshine" ending. We realize that David was an imperfect person just like we are. Yet we see a real intimacy in the love relationship David had with God. Along his life path, David had learned how to worship God. We see the many aspects of this through his psalms.

Israel's Singer of Songs

One cannot understand David's life without looking at his psalms! The secret to David's heart and his success in life was his relationship to God. We see this played out for us in the songs he wrote. What an interesting combination of qualities resided in this person: he could fight like a world champion, yet he knew how to worship with an open, tender heart toward God.

The songs David wrote were signposts throughout his life. We see the myriad of his life events through his songs. They seem to say to us, "This is what I am experiencing right now."

We see David sang in times of danger:

LORD, how many are my foes! How many rise up against me! Many are saying of me, "God will not deliver him." But you, LORD, are a shield around me, my

Switchbacks

glory, the One who lifts my head high. call out to the LORD, and he answers me from his holy mountain. (Psalm 3:1-4)

In times of despair:

My God, my God, why have you forsaken me? Why are you so far from saving me, so far from my cries of anguish? My God, I cry out by day, but you do not answer, by night, but I find no rest. Yet you are enthroned as the Holy One; you are the one Israel praises. In you our ancestors put their trust; they trusted and you delivered them. To you they cried out and were saved; in you they trusted and were not put to shame.

But I am a worm and not a man, scorned by everyone, despised by the people. All who see me mock me; they hurl insults, shaking their heads. "He trusts in the LORD," they say, "let the LORD rescue him. Let him deliver him, since he delights in him." (Psalm 22:1-8)

Praying for vindication and justice:

Contend, LORD, with those who contend with me; fight against those who fight against me. Take up shield and armor; arise and come to my aid. Brandish spear and javelin against those who pursue me. Say to me, "I am your salvation." (Psalm 35:1-3)

In repentance:

Have mercy on me, O God, according to your unfailing love; according to your great compassion blot out my transgressions. Wash away all my iniquity and cleanse me from my sin.

For I know my transgressions, and my sin is always before me. Against you, you only, have I sinned and done what is evil in your sight; so you are right in your verdict and justified when you judge. (Psalm 51:1-4)

In humility:

My heart is not proud, LORD, my eyes are not haughty; I do not concern myself with great matters or things too wonderful for me. But I have calmed and quieted myself, I am like a weaned child with its mother; like a weaned child I am content. Israel, put your hope in the Lord both now and forevermore. (Psalm 131)

In times of sickness:

All my enemies whisper together against me; they imagine the worst for me, saying, "A vile disease has afflicted him; he will never get up from the place where he lies." Even my close friend, someone I trusted, one who shared my bread, has turned against me.

But may you have mercy on me, LORD; raise me up, that I may repay them. I know that you are pleased with me, for my enemy does not triumph over me. (Psalm 41:7-11)

In times of joy and triumph:

My heart, O God, is steadfast; I will sing and make music with all my soul. Awake, harp and lyre! I will awaken the dawn. I will praise you, LORD, among the nations; I will sing of you among the peoples. For great is your love, higher than the heavens; your faithfulness reaches to the skies. Be exalted, O God, above the heavens; let your glory be over all the earth. (Psalm 108:1-5)

In times of resting in God's protection and provision:

The LORD is my shepherd, I lack nothing. He makes me lie down in green pastures, he leads me beside quiet waters, he refreshes my soul. He guides me along the right paths for his name's sake. Even though I walk through the darkest valley, I will fear no evil, for you are with me; your rod and your staff, they comfort me. You prepare a table before me in the presence of my enemies. You anoint my head with oil; my cup overflows. Surely your goodness and love will follow me all the days of my life, and I will dwell in the house of the LORD forever. (Psalm 23)

In the New Testament book of Acts, in a sermon Paul delivered in Pisidian Antioch, Paul described David as "a man after God's own heart." (Acts 13:22) This is perhaps most evident in the songs he sang to his Lord. And we also see that in many ways, David's experiences foreshadow those of Jesus Himself – the Son of David. Jesus too found great consolation in the psalms of his ancestor.

The End of the Line

David's death is recorded in just two verses:

Then David rested with his ancestors and was buried in the City of David. He had reigned forty years over Israel—seven years in Hebron and thirty-three in Jerusalem. (I Kings 2:10-11)

But that doesn't tell the whole story. What can we learn from this amazing life?

- God chose David, and that was the starting point. This made all the difference. He saw something in him – a heart for God. The Lord actually created David's heart. God chooses us, too, and Scripture tells us that we are greater than David, or any of the great Old Testament men or women! (Matthew 11:11)

- One word comes to my mind when looking at the life of David, and it describes his relationship to God. He was *genuine*. David really loved God. He loved God not only for what He did, but for who He was. He loved being in God's presence and enjoying fellowship with the Creator. Theirs was a love relationship that lasted a lifetime. Although he was a great warrior, he ultimately realized his victory and success was God's doing and not his own. Can it be any different for us?

- Just because of God's love for David and his love for God, things did not go smoothly or directly. David's journey to kingship was a long, uphill road – and this was God's will. Testing, refining, and learning were all part of David's long life as a fugitive from Saul and a victim of injustice. Evil and pain are a reality – God does not prevent these things from happening, but He protects His own through these times.

- David's "point of departure" for interpreting life situations was the Lord, not his circumstances. Take David's contest with Goliath, for example. He did not see his own smallness and the bigness of Goliath; he saw the bigness of his God and Goliath's insignificance. We would do well to have this same mindset in the face of the "giants" we face.

- Sometimes in David's life, God worked out his plan in spite of David's sin. The warning from this man's life is that just because we are righteous today is no guarantee we will be righteous tomorrow. We are all sinners capable of great evil. Life is complicated, and we make it even more so with our own sinful choices. Certainly, God did not lead David to sin with Bathsheba or to lose his temper over Nabal's insults. Sometimes the "crooked paths" in our lives are self-inflicted. But God works out His plan in spite of us, and His purposes and amazing grace are the overriding factor.

- The gift of music is a wonderful avenue for coming close to God. I wonder what David's life would have looked like if not for music. Throughout his life, it helped him make sense out of the tumult and strife, and led him back to God. Music reaches the heart in ways that few things in creation can. It even soothed the heart and mind of the wicked King Saul, and it can minister to us, too.

Jesus said, *"In this world, you will have trouble, ..."* (John 16:33) David probably would have shouted "Amen!" to these words. Another hymn writer generations later, Annie S. Hawks, would put it this way:

> *I need thee ev'ry hour, Most gracious Lord. No tender voice like thine Can peace afford. I need thee, oh, I need thee; Ev'ry hour I need thee! Oh, bless me now, my Savior; I come to thee!*

Questions for Reflection and Discussion

1. Reflect upon David's humble beginnings – the eighth son of a common shepherd. How did David remember his humble origins throughout his life, and when did he forget them?

2. We read that the Spirit of the Lord came upon David as a young man. What events in his life showed that God was with him?

3. David was extremely patient in many trials throughout his life, and yet there were times when he lost his patience. Can you think of such times of failure in his life? How can you relate to David's weaknesses?

4. David faced great injustice at the hands of King Saul. How did he handle such poor treatment? What lessons are in this action for you?

5. There were times in David's life when individuals were channels of God's grace toward David. Reflect upon the influences of Jonathan, Abigail, and perhaps others during his times of utmost need. Are there people in your life that God has used in a similar manner?

6. David's potential catastrophe at the burning of Ziklag and at several other times in his life caused him to run to God. What is your reaction to difficult circumstances you face?

7. Music, "journaling," and poetry seemed to be outlets and lifelines for David throughout his life. What activities get you through hard times?

David Rox

Switchbacks

8

A Tale of Two Mountains: ELIJAH

"What are you doing here, Elijah?" (I Kings 19:9)

On the Mount of Transfiguration in Matthew 17, there were two figures who appeared with Jesus – Moses and Elijah. Why Elijah? Who did he represent in the history of Israel? He was a prophet that called the people back, who reminded them of God's covenant and love. His message paved a way of return and fellowship with God.

He was also a great miracle worker among the prophets, and his words were confirmed by miraculous actions. His story was even immortalized in an oratorio by Felix Mendelssohn. He was a man of action – a man very zealous for the Lord. His life was so marked with miracles that in the end, he was taken by a flaming chariot to heaven! He is one of only two biblical characters who never tasted death. Biblical prophecy talks about his return before the coming of the Messiah. To this day, Jewish people leave an empty seat at the Passover table for the prophet Elijah, should he come. He is an important figure, indeed!

And yet, he was a human being just like us. His life was often hard and full of disappointment and even depression. And like David, failures in faith followed great spiritual victories. This is one of the points of this book: our lives are not free from zigs and zags or temptations and trials. But God is blazing His winding trail in our lives by His power and grace.

The Rainless Reign of Ahab

It had been less than 200 years since the golden age of King David and Solomon. Israel had experienced a split into the Northern and Southern Kingdoms. Israel in the north had a more tumultuous history than its southern neighbor Judah. There had been several kingly lines and assassinations, while as God had promised, David's royal line had remained intact in the southern kingdom.

At the beginning of this story, King Ahab was reigning in the northern capital city of Samaria. He was an evil man.

> *Ahab son of Omri did more evil in the eyes of the LORD than any of those before him. He not only considered it trivial to commit the sins of Jeroboam son of Nebat, but he also married Jezebel daughter of Ethbaal king of the Sidonians, and began to serve Baal and worship him. He set up an altar for Baal in the temple of Baal that he built in Samaria. Ahab also made an Asherah pole and did more to arouse the anger of the LORD, the God of Israel, than did all the kings of Israel before him. (I Kings 16:30-33)*

During these wicked days, in stepped Elijah, God's prophet. He was a Tishbite from Gilead, and he had a message for Ahab.

> *"As the LORD, the God of Israel, lives, whom I serve, there will be neither dew nor rain in the next few years except at my word." (I Kings 17:1)*

This declaration was quite an affront to Baal, the fertility god. Baal was supposed to bless the land with rain and good crops, and Elijah's declaration challenged this belief. The lack of rain should have convinced Ahab and the people of Israel that Baal had no real power – that he was a false god.

Elijah delivered this unpopular message and then God told him to hide in the Kerith ravine east of the Jordan River. Elijah spoke for the Lord and then fled to the wilderness – he was a hit and run prophet. There God promised to give him water to drink from Kerith Brook and he would be fed by ravens.

God was good at his word – there was a tremendous drought that hit Israel, and yet Elijah was provided for. God was punishing the entire Northern Kingdom for the sin of King Ahab. Many good people suffered because of this natural calamity. We see here an illustration of an important truth: leaders' sins affect many people. Therefore, we should pray for our leaders – even the evil ones!

God provided for Elijah, but he did not enjoy four-star accommodations. Eventually the drought was so severe that even the Kerith Brook dried up. Elijah experienced discomfort along with his countrymen. In earthly terms and using human logic, Elijah's dilemma was his own fault, and the fault of his God. Elijah's problem came about because he was right smack dab in the center of God's will for his life!

At any rate, the Lord told him to leave that region and go to stay with a widow in the pagan town of Zarephath – with a Gentile woman living in modern-day Lebanon.

Switchbacks

Elijah probably went to this foreign land because he was a fugitive fleeing from King Ahab. Like David was forced to do, Elijah was hiding. This Gentile widow reminds me of Ruth, and how God wove a foreign woman into the biblical story. God's heart has always been for the nations.

Once again, staying with the widow of Zarephath proved to be far less than four-star accommodations. When Elijah met her, the widow was down to her last meal, and was preparing it for herself and her starving son. But she was willing to share it with Elijah. The prophet told her not to be afraid, but God would miraculously supply food for them all until the rains came. And God again proved Himself good at His word. Her meager larder never ran out!

But sometime later, more trouble arose. The widow's only son became ill and eventually died. The woman cried out to the prophet in her own home:

> *"What do you have against me, man of God? Did you come to remind me of my sin and kill my son?" (I Kings 17:18)*

Elijah then performed one of the most remarkable miracles in the Old Testament. He took the dead boy and quite literally laid the matter before the Lord.

> *"Give me your son," Elijah replied. He took him from her arms, carried him to the upper room where he was staying, and laid him on his bed. Then he cried out to the LORD, "LORD my God, have you brought tragedy even on this widow I am staying with, by causing her son to die?" Then he stretched himself out on the boy three times and cried out to the LORD, "LORD my God, let this boy's life return to him!"*
>
> *The LORD heard Elijah's cry, and the boy's life returned to him, and he lived. Elijah picked up the child and carried him down from the room into the house. He gave him to his mother and said, "Look, your son is alive!"*
>
> *Then the woman said to Elijah, "Now I know that you are a man of God and that the word of the LORD from your mouth is the truth." (I Kings 17:19-24)*

Not only was Elijah a miracle worker, but he proved himself to be a man of fervent prayer. We shall see this again when he later prayed for the drought to finally end.

Let's Have a Contest

During the third year of the drought proclaimed by Elijah, the Lord told his prophet to return to Ahab's court. This was a dangerous proposition, but Elijah obeyed. Remarkable! It would have been like David going to visit King Saul while the King was hunting him. And have you noticed how often God's selected servants became "Public Enemy Number One?" For example: Moses, David, Elijah, Paul and even Jesus. While on his way to Samaria, Elijah learned from a godly palace administrator named Obadiah that Ahab had been scouring the land looking for him with the intent of killing him. It was more than apparent the long drought had not softened Ahab's heart. When Elijah finally met Ahab, the King greeted God's prophet with the words: *"Is that you, you troubler of Israel?"* (I Kings 18:17)

Elijah gave it right back to his king, and spoke boldly to this ungodly monarch.

> *"I have not made trouble for Israel," Elijah replied. "But you and your father's family have. You have abandoned the LORD's commands and have followed the Baals." (I Kings 18:18)*

Elijah then gave orders to Ahab. This in itself was bravery beyond belief! He told him to summon all the people of Israel to Mount Carmel, and to gather all the pagan prophets of Baal and Asherah – 850 in all, who ate at Queen Jezabel's table. Elijah was about to hold a rather lopsided contest between the God of Israel and Baal and Asherah. He would be the sole prophet of the Lord, and would face down 850 counterfeit priests.

Elijah's boldness and righteous indignation were similar to that of the young boy David when he met Goliath. He did not focus upon the size of his opposition, but rather he viewed only the total sovereignty and power of his God. Elijah was not small compared to all those false prophets of Baal – they were small compared to the Lord.

Surprisingly, Ahab obeyed Elijah, and the contest was on. The story is such a good one, I have included it below in its entirety.

> *Elijah went before the people and said, "How long will you waver between two opinions? If the LORD is God, follow him; but if Baal is God, follow him." But the people said nothing.*
>
> *Then Elijah said to them, "I am the only one of the LORD's prophets left, but Baal has four hundred and fifty prophets. Get two bulls for us. Let Baal's prophets choose one for themselves, and let them cut it into pieces and put it on the wood but not set fire to it. I will prepare the other bull and put it on the wood*

but not set fire to it. Then you call on the name of your god, and I will call on the name of the LORD. The god who answers by fire—he is God."

Then all the people said, "What you say is good."

Elijah said to the prophets of Baal, "Choose one of the bulls and prepare it first, since there are so many of you. Call on the name of your god, but do not light the fire." So they took the bull given them and prepared it.

Then they called on the name of Baal from morning till noon. "Baal, answer us!" they shouted. But there was no response; no one answered. And they danced around the altar they had made.

At noon Elijah began to taunt them. "Shout louder!" he said. "Surely he is a god! Perhaps he is deep in thought, or busy, or traveling. Maybe he is sleeping and must be awakened." So they shouted louder and slashed themselves with swords and spears, as was their custom, until their blood flowed. Midday passed, and they continued their frantic prophesying until the time for the evening sacrifice. But there was no response, no one answered, no one paid attention.

Then Elijah said to all the people, "Come here to me." They came to him, and he repaired the altar of the LORD, which had been torn down. Elijah took twelve stones, one for each of the tribes descended from Jacob, to whom the word of the LORD had come, saying, "Your name shall be Israel." With the stones he built an altar in the name of the LORD, and he dug a trench around it large enough to hold two seahs of seed. He arranged the wood, cut the bull into pieces and laid it on the wood. Then he said to them, "Fill four large jars with water and pour it on the offering and on the wood."

"Do it again," he said, and they did it again. "Do it a third time," he ordered, and they did it the third time. The water ran down around the altar and even filled the trench.

At the time of sacrifice, the prophet Elijah stepped forward and prayed: "LORD, the God of Abraham, Isaac and Israel, let it be known today that you are God in Israel and that I am your servant and have done all these things at your command. Answer me, LORD, answer me, so these people will know that you, LORD, are God, and that you are turning their hearts back again."

> *Then the fire of the LORD fell and burned up the sacrifice, the wood, the stones and the soil, and also licked up the water in the trench. When all the people saw this, they fell prostrate and cried, "The LORD—he is God! The LORD—he is God!"*
>
> *Then Elijah commanded them, "Seize the prophets of Baal. Don't let anyone get away!" They seized them, and Elijah had them brought down to the Kishon Valley and slaughtered there. (I Kings 18:21-40)*

We must admire the sincerity and the passion with which the prophets of Baal worshipped their god. However, faith is validated not by its amount, but rather by its object. Great faith misplaced is worthless. In the end, Elijah's humble prayer got answered, while the bloody rants of the masses fell upon deaf ears. As my former pastor, Harold Bussell, used to say, "We do not have to have great faith in God, but rather faith in a great God."

The contest on Mount Carmel is one of the most heroic sagas in the Old Testament. Elijah's passion was to call the people of Israel back to their God. After the "victory celebration," Elijah told King Ahab that rain would finally return. He prayed persistently and passionately for God to break the drought and send rain, and the Lord answered his request. The contest was over and the rains came.

Jezebel's wrath

We might think Elijah's story could end happily here, and he would be proclaimed a hero and redeemer of Israel. But this was not the case. As cynics are fond of saying, "no good deed goes unpunished."

Scripture frequently shows when a work of God is making a difference, opposition soon arises. And "hell hath no fury . . . ."

> *Now Ahab told Jezebel everything Elijah had done and how he had killed all the prophets with the sword. So Jezebel sent a messenger to Elijah to say, "May the gods deal with me, be it ever so severely, if by this time tomorrow I do not make your life like that of one of them." (I Kings 19:1-2)*

Elijah's courage and boldness melted away. He became afraid and ran for his life. How could he do this? Just earlier on Mount Carmel he faced a host of false prophets and viewed them as nothing compared to his God. Now, one woman – a wicked queen – sends him running for his life. It reminds me of David, who as a young boy killed Goliath and relied upon God's strength, yet as an old man he wanted to rely on strength of numbers and counted his troops through a census. David forgot his strength came from the Lord, not humans. And Elijah forgot this, too!

He fled south into the Desert of Beersheba and sat dejectedly under a broom tree. There he prayed that he might die.

> "I have had enough, LORD," he said. "Take my life; I am no better than my ancestors." Then he lay down under the bush and fell asleep. (I Kings 19:4-5)

This sounds like a classic case of depression. If it is not, it certainly looks and sounds like Elijah was indulging in some serious self-pity. He was ready to quit as a prophet of God. Like Naomi generations earlier, Elijah had given up hope. Perhaps he believed his life's path to be over, ending in desolation.

But God had other plans.

Elijah was awakened suddenly by an angel of God, and found a hearty meal had been prepared for him. He ate and then laid down again to continue his exhausted, depressed sleep. The angel appeared a second time and woke him again. Another heavenly meal was waiting for him. I had never noticed before that God graciously provided two heavenly meals for Elijah. He was twice blessed, and God was incredibly patient with the self-pitying prophet. Elijah was ordered to eat, because the journey ahead of him was a long one. He was to travel forty days and forty nights to Mount Horeb (Sinai), the mountain of God. So Elijah was called to a second mountain. He made the journey to this holy place and settled in a cave – perhaps one of the same caves in which Moses himself spent time when receiving God's laws for Israel.

Elijah meets God

After getting some restorative sleep, the Lord appeared to Elijah on the mountain. God's first words to him were in the form of a question:

> "What are you doing here, Elijah?" (I Kings 19:9)

Implied in this question, I think, was that Elijah was wrong to run from Jezebel. Why would a man who could face down hundreds of pagan priests and prophets and call down fire from heaven fear one wicked queen? Somehow, he had taken his eyes off of God and fixed them on his earthly circumstances. Elijah showed himself to be human, after all – just like us.

The prophet answered this question with some words that almost sound like a rehearsed speech he had played like a recording over and over in his head:

> *"I have been very zealous for the LORD God Almighty. The Israelites have rejected your covenant, torn down your altars, and put your prophets to death with the sword. I am the only one left, and now they are trying to kill me too." (I Kings 19:10)*

Elijah thought he had answered God's question in a satisfactory way, but we are not so sure. God's answer to Elijah's plight was not to sympathize with his situation, but to reveal Himself to his prophet in a new and powerful way. Like in Job's story, the answer to Elijah's problems was simply seeing God in a new light – getting a greater glimpse of Him.

> *The LORD said, "Go out and stand on the mountain in the presence of the LORD, for the LORD is about to pass by." (I Kings 19:11)*

A great wind passed by and tore the rocks from the mountain. This was followed by an earthquake and then a great fire, but the Lord Himself was not present in any of these terrifying, mighty signs. This trio of natural disasters was then followed by a still small voice – a gentle whisper. In this gentle whisper, the Lord repeated the question:

> *"What are you doing here, Elijah?" (I Kings 19:13)*

This was such a penetrating question. God asked it twice. *"What are you doing here, Elijah?"* It is an odd question for God to ask once, let alone twice. After all, God had told him to travel to Mt. Sinai. On the surface, that is why Elijah was there. But God was asking Elijah where he was *mentally* and *spiritually*. The Lord was getting to the heart of Elijah's problem by asking this question. Implied in the question was God's answer. God was with Elijah. He had proven Himself sufficient in the face of drought, famine, and strong opposition. Now one godless woman sent him running for his life in fear. Why was he running? Why indeed! What was Jezebel in light of the wind, earthquake and fire he had just witnessed?

God could have asked the same question to other Biblical figures at times in their lives. Like Abraham, after he had given his wife away to Pharaoh, saying she was his sister. Or to King David, that one spring night when he committed adultery with Bathsheba. Or Moses, when he struck the rock to bring forth water in his rage. What were they doing there in those places?

Switchbacks

God's question to Elijah was a gracious, non-condemning one. His desire was to bring his servant back to focus on spiritual reality. And so it is with us. Might we need to hear God's still small voice saying to us, *"What are you doing here?"* God is sovereign and more powerful than any person or any dangerous situation. We can trust Him and we can stand firm rather than cave in. We can receive strength to go forward.

By asking the same question twice, perhaps God was giving Elijah a chance to revise his answer in light of the powerful display he has just witnessed. Whatever God's reasons, Elijah played the pre-recorded tape for the Lord once again.

"I have been very zealous for the LORD God Almighty. The Israelites have rejected your covenant, torn down your altars, and put your prophets to death with the sword. I am the only one left, and now they are trying to kill me too."
(I Kings 19:14)

Look at Elijah's perspective on his situation. His view of reality was less than accurate. There were elements of truth in his response to God. He had been very zealous for the Lord. He had worked very hard as God's representative, and he was worn out. Perhaps zeal was not all Elijah needed. He needed to do less and see God more. He needed to slow down and listen for God's gentle whisper.

Elijah was right on a second point, too. Most of his nation had rejected God's covenant and turned to wickedness. And Queen Jezebel was trying to kill him now. But he was wrong when he stated that he alone was left among the faithful. His perspective was partly true, but fatally flawed.

Elijah's focus was what ours would be in his situation – he saw only his immediate circumstances and he felt trapped by them. Gaining God's perspective seemed far out of his grasp. Graciously, the Lord did not rebuke him for being a faithless blockhead, but rather He put His prophet back to work. The Lord gave Elijah a list of tasks to perform, reminding him he was still the Lord's servant. He was to go back the way he came, to anoint a man king over the foreign country of Aram, to anoint a new king over Israel to replace Ahab, and to commission his replacement, the young prophet Elisha. God also corrected Elijah's wrong thinking when he claimed that he was the only godly person left in Israel. There were in fact 7,000 people faithful to the Lord and on Elijah's side. Notice what it says in I Kings 19:18: *"Yet I reserve 7000 in Israel – all whose knees have not bowed down to Baal."* This is not a huge number, but it was enough for Elijah to realize God was still at work in Israel. God had made "reservations" – he still kept 7,000 faithful! God sealed and protected a remnant He called His own. What might this say to us in our 21st Century America? Do we get discouraged about where our culture is, and that we seem to see our world going to hell in a handbasket? Is there still a remnant faithful to God in our post-Christian culture? Yes! God does not leave Himself without a witness.

The Lord's approach seemed to work with Elijah. He had had a fresh encounter with God, and he left Mount Horeb revitalized and ready to carry out God's work once again.

After completing these three assigned tasks, Elijah's powerful ministry was almost over. He appears briefly in I Kings 21, where he confronted wicked King Ahab yet again for killing an innocent man and stealing his vineyard. Elijah's boldness continued to be a thorn in Ahab's side!

In II Kings 1, King Ahab had been killed in a battle, and his wicked son Ahaziah had taken his place. Ahaziah had fallen and hurt himself severely, and had inquired of foreign gods about whether or not he would recover from his injuries. An angel appeared to Elijah and instructed him to send a message of judgement to Ahaziah:

> *The angel of the LORD said to Elijah the Tishbite, "Go up and meet the messengers of the king of Samaria and ask them, 'Is it because there is no God in Israel that you are going off to consult Baal-Zebub, the god of Ekron?' Therefore this is what the LORD says: 'You will not leave the bed you are lying on. You will certainly die!'" (II Kings 1:3-4)*

When King Ahaziah received Elijah's prophetic message, he sent soldiers to order Elijah to appear before him. Two times he sent a contingent of fifty soldiers, and two times Elijah called down fire from heaven to consume them. It appears that Elijah still had the knack for being the prophet of fire, just as he had during the contest on Mount Carmel years earlier. A third unfortunate captain was sent to retrieve Elijah, but he humbly begged for mercy.

> *The king sent a third captain with his fifty men. This third captain went up and fell on his knees before Elijah. "Man of God," he begged, "please have respect for my life and the lives of these fifty men, your servants! See, fire has fallen from heaven and consumed the first two captains and all their men. But now have respect for my life!"*
>
> *The angel of the LORD said to Elijah, "Go down with him; do not be afraid of him." So Elijah got up and went down with him to the king. (II Kings 1:13-15)*

Elijah's prophecy came true, and the wicked King Ahaziah did die from his injuries, ushering in a new chapter in the history of the Northern Kingdom of Israel. We read that after Elijah completed this task, it was time for him to depart this earth. And what a departure! The Lord eventually took him up into heaven in a fiery chariot.

The End of the Line

Like all of God's prophets, Elijah was chosen by God for a time and purpose. This person was sent to call others back to the Lord and to remind them of God's covenant with Israel. At times, he must have felt like a car salesman who is trying to sell a Cadillac to people who don't even know what a car is!

Although our callings might not be as lofty as Elijah's, there are lessons here for us.

- Elijah's mission was not an easy one. Obeying God's will meant suffering hunger, thirst, rejection, danger, and opposition. When he declared there would be no rain, that affected his food supply along with everyone else's. Following God's plan for our lives will often lead us and those we love into times of discomfort, suffering and even persecution. When God is at work, the Enemy will always mount an opposition. The Apostle Paul promised as much: *In fact, everyone who wants to live a godly life in Christ Jesus will be persecuted.* (II Timothy 3:12)

- In our lives, spiritual victories and defeats often follow close on the heels of one another. Elijah did not shrink from the formidable odds on Mount Carmel, and stood up to the opposition in a most courageous way. However, in the face of opposition after a great victory, he showed his weakness and fear by running from Jezebel. He might have expected God to provide straighter, easier paths for him after Mount Carmel, but God had other plans.

- Along every step, God supplied Elijah with what he needed, if not with what he wanted. Remember, at one point he wanted to die! When he was at his lowest point, God gave him a glimpse of Himself on Mount Horeb in a still small voice. God gives us what we need, but not always what we want.

- Part of Elijah's "pre-recorded" speech to God included his statement that he had been "very zealous" for the Lord. Apparently, zeal wasn't everything he needed, and the same may be true for us. There may be times in life when we need to stop doing things for the Lord and simply ask to see His glory. Instead of asking,

"Lord, what do you want me to do?" We might ask instead, *"Lord, who do you want me to be?"*

- In his dejected state, Elijah falsely believed he was alone in serving God. Like Naomi, Elijah felt like God had deserted him. Sometimes we feel alone and forgotten, too. But God did not leave Himself without witnesses in Naomi's or Elijah's life, and neither does He in our lives. Feelings of loneliness are part of our human experience, but they are just that – feelings. God continues to work His purpose out, and His purpose cannot be thwarted.

- Finally, God graciously redirected Elijah to complete his work, even in the midst of his self-pity and depression. There was a light at the end of the tunnel for Elijah, and work left for him to do. In the midst of our trials and darkest times, He will provide light for us as well. As long as we remain alive, God has work for us to do.

A key in Elijah's life was fervent prayer. We are reminded of this in the New Testament by James.

> *The effective, fervent prayer of a righteous man avails much. Elijah was a man with a nature like ours, and he prayed earnestly that it would not rain; and it did not rain on the land for three years and six months. And he prayed again, and the heaven gave rain, and the earth produced its fruit. (James 5:16-17)*

At the end of Elijah's life, loose ends abounded. There was political intrigue and turmoil throughout the region. Israel still struggled with idolatry and wicked rulers. Yet, God was working his purpose out in this man's life, as He is today in our lives!

And remarkably, in the pages of Scripture we learn that we may not have heard the last of Elijah. He may reappear one day in the future.

Questions for Reflection and Discussion

1. Elijah, as God's prophet, was asked to do frightening things, like stand up to a wicked king and face down hundreds of false prophets and priests of pagan deities. How do you react to intimidating circumstances?

2. Elijah became "Public Enemy Number One" because he obeyed God. Have you ever suffered persecution of any kind because of your actions for God?

3. Obeying God often meant choosing discomfort over security for Elijah. Can you cite instances in his life story where this was the case? How might you respond if God were to call you in a similar fashion?

4. What was the nature of Elijah's prayers that we have recorded in his story? What can we learn about prayer from his example?

5. At times Elijah was bold, and at other times his courage left him. What possible explanation is there for this inconsistency? Can you relate to his sudden loss of courage in the face of evil?

6. Elijah suffered from a type of depression and gave in to self-pity. How did this cloud his judgment regarding his circumstances? How did God bring him out of this "dark place?" How might God deal with you in similar times?

7. Elijah thought he was alone, but God did not leave himself without a witness, and corrected the prophet's understanding of reality. How is this true today as well?

David Rox

Switchbacks

9

Walking With Courage: DANIEL

"I am sending you out like sheep among wolves. Therefore be as shrewd as snakes and as innocent as doves." (Matthew 10:16)

Uprooted and Replanted

How would you feel if you became a human "spoil of war?"

Like with Job, the book of Daniel begins with catastrophe – Jerusalem was besieged, defeated, and looted. We can ask the same question we did when looking at Job: *"What do you do when life falls off a cliff?"*

Daniel must have been from the upper crust in Hebrew society and was of prime interest to Jerusalem's conquerors. He was of high birth, a young man, well-educated, handsome, and without any defect. He was bright and teachable. The Babylonians saw this young man as a real prize. He was to be useful to the empire and absorbed into their culture. But little did the Babylonians know, Daniel was ultimately to be used by God for His divine purposes.

The process of Babylonian absorption was a standard one. Once Daniel was carted off he was subjected to a three-year indoctrination process. On the surface, this was not too bad. Daniel and three of his fellow Hebrew companions were to be well-fed and completely taken care of. They were, however, renamed by their captors. Daniel, whose name means "God is my judge" was renamed Belteshazar; Hananiah (meaning "The Lord shows grace") was renamed Shadrach; Mishael (meaning "Who is what God is?") was renamed Meshach; and Azariah (meaning "The Lord helps") was renamed Abednego. New names meant that they were under new authority and were expected to take on new identities; their pagan names were undoubtedly tied to honoring Babylonian deities.

Daniel and his comrades had a critical decision to make early on in their new lives: they were required by the royal Babylonian officials to eat food declared unclean in the law of Moses. Would they "go with the flow" or hold on to their Hebrew traditions? We read early on in the story what they decided to do:

> *But Daniel resolved not to defile himself with the royal food and wine, and he asked the chief official for permission not to defile himself this way. (Daniel 1:8)*

Like Joseph in Egypt, Daniel and his friends had found favor with the supervising Gentiles in their lives. They stood out from their peers and had great wisdom and understanding. Arioch, a head official of the king who was in charge of Daniel and all the other men being groomed for the court, showed sympathy towards these young Hebrews – at great risk to himself. Daniel used wisdom and tact, and suggested an alternative diet and a test. Rather than simply rebelling and going on a starvation diet, he proposed a ten-day vegetarian diet for the four men. God caused this plan to succeed.

After three years of indoctrination, Daniel and his three friends excelled above all others, and they became the king's favorites.

> *In every matter of wisdom and understanding about which the king questioned them, he found them ten times better than all the magicians and enchanters in his whole kingdom. (Daniel 1:20)*

Thanks to God's blessing, these were extraordinary men. Daniel was to remain in various pagan governments as a chief royal advisor and administrator for almost seventy years.

A Hothead King

King Nebuchadnezzar of Babylon was a tough boss. In the second chapter of the book of Daniel, we read he had a dream that troubled him deeply. He wanted to know its meaning, but he did not want to be tricked by anyone in his court. Therefore, he decided he would not even tell anyone the content of his dream. He required that an enchanter tell him exactly what he dreamt and then interpret its meaning. And to make matters worse, Nebuchadnezzar threatened all his officials with death and total destruction of their homes if they could not give him the answers he demanded.

The aides all declared:

> *What the king asks is too difficult. No one can reveal it to the king except the gods, and they do not live among humans. (Daniel 2:11)*

When Nebuchadnezzar heard this response, he decided to put all his wise men to death – a rather harsh decree! When one served a king like this, one's life hung by a thread every day. Daniel and his friends were sentenced to death with all the other officials and enchanters, but once again Daniel thought quickly and wisely, and then acted with courage.

> *When Arioch, the commander of the king's guard, had gone out to put to death the wise men of Babylon, Daniel spoke to him with wisdom and tact. He asked the king's officer, "Why did the king issue such a harsh decree?" Arioch then explained the matter to Daniel. At this, Daniel went in to the king and asked for time, so that he might interpret the dream for him. (Daniel 2:14-16)*

Imagine going to a hothead like the king and asking for more time! Daniel and his three friends then prayed to God for deliverance, and God answered by revealing Nebuchadnezzar's dream to Daniel that night in a vision.

Upon receiving an answer to his prayer, Daniel praised and thanked his God.

> *Praise be to the name of God for ever and ever; wisdom and power are his. He changes times and seasons; he deposes kings and raises up others. He gives wisdom to the wise and knowledge to the discerning. He reveals deep and hidden things; he knows what lies in darkness, and light dwells with him. I thank and praise you, God of my ancestors: You have given me wisdom and power, you have made known to me what we asked of you, you have made known to us the dream of the king. (Daniel 2:20-23)*

Daniel reported to the king's official Arioch that executions could be stayed for everyone, because he could fulfill the king's request. The young Hebrew man was then brought before the great and angry King of Babylon.

> *The king asked Daniel (also called Belteshazzar), "Are you able to tell me what I saw in my dream and interpret it?"*
>
> *Daniel replied, "No wise man, enchanter, magician or diviner can explain to the king the mystery he has asked about, but there is a God in heaven who reveals mysteries. He has shown King Nebuchadnezzar what will happen in days to come. Your dream and the visions that passed through your mind as you were lying in bed are these:"*

"As Your Majesty was lying there, your mind turned to things to come, and the revealer of mysteries showed you what is going to happen. As for me, this mystery has been revealed to me, not because I have greater wisdom than anyone else alive, but so that Your Majesty may know the interpretation and that you may understand what went through your mind."

"Your Majesty looked, and there before you stood a large statue—an enormous, dazzling statue, awesome in appearance. The head of the statue was made of pure gold, its chest and arms of silver, its belly and thighs of bronze, its legs of iron, its feet partly of iron and partly of baked clay. While you were watching, a rock was cut out, but not by human hands. It struck the statue on its feet of iron and clay and smashed them. Then the iron, the clay, the bronze, the silver and the gold were all broken to pieces and became like chaff on a threshing floor in the summer. The wind swept them away without leaving a trace. But the rock that struck the statue became a huge mountain and filled the whole earth." (Daniel 2:26-35)

Daniel was able to do what no magician or enchanter in Babylon was capable of doing. He told Nebuchadnezzar his dream and then interpreted it. God had given the pagan king a vision of the future rise and fall of several kingdoms – starting with his own and followed by a series of lesser empires, until the establishment of an eternal kingdom established by God. This final kingdom would obliterate all empires that came before it.

In interpreting the king's dream, Daniel did not take the credit himself. He humbly gave the credit of this knowledge to God. In this way, he acted exactly as Joseph did when that young man interpreted Pharoah's dreams foretelling the famine to take place throughout the region so long ago (Genesis 41:16).

Understandably, Nebuchadnezzar was impressed. And when this king was impressed, he acted in an all-out fashion.

Then King Nebuchadnezzar fell prostrate before Daniel and paid him honor and ordered that an offering and incense be presented to him. The king said to Daniel, "Surely your God is the God of gods and the Lord of kings and a revealer of mysteries, for you were able to reveal this mystery."

Then the king placed Daniel in a high position and lavished many gifts on him. He made him ruler over the entire province of Babylon and placed him in charge of all its wise men. Moreover, at Daniel's request the king appointed Shadrach, Meshach and Abednego administrators over the province of Babylon, while Daniel himself remained at the royal court. (Daniel 2:46-49)

But serving a mercurial, impulsive king like this was dangerous business, as Daniel's three friends soon found out. Serving these pagan monarchs even made Jacob's serving his "bad boss" Uncle Laban look like a field day.

The Fiery Furnace

Daniel and his godly friends were blessed to serve in positions of great authority, and no doubt they did so extremely well. But with this blessing came dangers. Like in any human government, one crisis seemed to follow another. Political jealousy among rivals, intrigue, envy and unbending edicts from egotistical, power-hungry heads of state all created problems. Godliness always meets with evil opposition, and this certainly is the case with Daniel and his friends.

For example, Nebuchadnezzar took his dream of the statue to heart in the wrong way, and built a statue of pure gold in his own honor. He then insisted everyone bow down to it. The story of Shadrach, Meshach and Abednego is the stuff of Old Testament legend. Nebuchadnezzar built a fiery furnace and threw these three disobedient, unbending Hebrew men into it, only to find that their God delivered them from the flames.

King Nebuchadnezzar was impressed, and made a typical despotic decree:

Then Nebuchadnezzar said, "Praise be to the God of Shadrach, Meshach and Abednego, who has sent his angel and rescued his servants! They trusted in him and defied the king's command and were willing to give up their lives rather than serve or worship any god except their own God. Therefore I decree that the people of any nation or language who say anything against the God of Shadrach, Meshach and Abednego be cut into pieces and their houses be turned into piles of rubble, for no other god can save in this way." (Daniel 2:28-29)

This king ran hot and cold.

Another Dream, Another King

Sometime later, Nebuchadnezzar had another disturbing dream – this time, about a tree that flourished for a time until cut down on the orders of heaven. The stump of the tree was bound for seven years before being allowed to start growing again.

And Daniel was called upon once again to interpret the dream. It was a hard message for the king to hear, but Daniel courageously delivered it – similar to the words of condemnation the prophet Elijah had to speak to wicked King Ahab years before.

> *This is the interpretation, Your Majesty, and this is the decree the Most High has issued against my lord the king: You will be driven away from people and will live with the wild animals; you will eat grass like the ox and be drenched with the dew of heaven. Seven times will pass by for you until you acknowledge that the Most High is sovereign over all kingdoms on earth and gives them to anyone he wishes. The command to leave the stump of the tree with its roots means that your kingdom will be restored to you when you acknowledge that Heaven rules. Therefore, Your Majesty, be pleased to accept my advice: Renounce your sins by doing what is right, and your wickedness by being kind to the oppressed. It may be that then your prosperity will continue. (Daniel 4:24-27)*

Daniel's warning fell upon deaf ears. But all he prophesied came true. Nebuchadnezzar was struck down and humbled for seven years until he acknowledged the God of Heaven. After this he was restored to his throne in Babylon. So God could even create winding paths for pagan kings to travel!

Nebuchadnezzar's reign resumed. But after his death, his son Belshazzar became king of Babylon, and suffered from the same flaws his father had. He also refused to acknowledge the God of Heaven and paid the price. He used the holy vessels from the temple of Jerusalem in one of his pagan feasts, and God's judgment fell upon him. The very night of the feast, a mysterious hand wrote a message on a plaster wall in the palace. After all the king's enchanters failed to discern the meaning of the writing, the old man Daniel was finally summoned to interpret the meaning of the writing on the wall.

King Belshazzar offered Daniel great rewards if he could interpret the writing, but Daniel refused these gifts. He then proceeded to give the new king a history lesson.

> *"Your Majesty, the Most High God gave your father Nebuchadnezzar sovereignty and greatness and glory and splendor. Because of the high position he gave him, all the nations and peoples of every language dreaded and feared*

him. Those the king wanted to put to death, he put to death; those he wanted to spare, he spared; those he wanted to promote, he promoted; and those he wanted to humble, he humbled. But when his heart became arrogant and hardened with pride, he was deposed from his royal throne and stripped of his glory. He was driven away from people and given the mind of an animal; he lived with the wild donkeys and ate grass like the ox; and his body was drenched with the dew of heaven, until he acknowledged that the Most High God is sovereign over all kingdoms on earth and sets over them anyone he wishes.

"But you, Belshazzar, his son, have not humbled yourself, though you knew all this. Instead, you have set yourself up against the Lord of heaven. You had the goblets from his temple brought to you, and you and your nobles, your wives and your concubines drank wine from them. You praised the gods of silver and gold, of bronze, iron, wood and stone, which cannot see or hear or understand. But you did not honor the God who holds in his hand your life and all your ways. Therefore he sent the hand that wrote the inscription.

"This is the inscription that was written: MENE, MENE, TEKEL, PARSIN

Here is what these words mean:

Mene: *God has numbered the days of your reign and brought it to an end.*

Tekel: *You have been weighed on the scales and found wanting.*

Peres: *Your kingdom is divided and given to the Medes and Persians."*

Then at Belshazzar's command, Daniel was clothed in purple, a gold chain was placed around his neck, and he was proclaimed the third highest ruler in the kingdom.

That very night Belshazzar, king of the Babylonians, was slain, and Darius the Mede took over the kingdom, at the age of sixty-two. (Daniel 5:18-30)

Belshazzar's generous reward to Daniel turned out to mean nothing, since the Babylonian king's reign ended that very night. Once again, Daniel faced an uncertain future. Would the new ruler, Darius the Mede, be better or worse than Daniel's old masters?

A Den of Lions

As Daniel entered his old age, he was still highly regarded by King Darius.

It pleased Darius to appoint 120 satraps to rule throughout the kingdom, with three administrators over them, one of whom was Daniel. The satraps were made accountable to them so that the king might not suffer loss. Now Daniel so distinguished himself among the administrators and the satraps by his exceptional qualities that the king planned to set him over the whole kingdom. At this, the administrators and the satraps tried to find grounds for charges against Daniel in his conduct of government affairs, but they were unable to do so. They could find no corruption in him, because he was trustworthy and neither corrupt nor negligent. Finally these men said, "We will never find any basis for charges against this man Daniel unless it has something to do with the law of his God." (Daniel 6:1-5)

Daniel was excellent in his service to this pagan king. And like his ancestor Joseph with the Egyptian Pharaoh, the ruler of the Medes and Persians planned to make him second only to himself. As might be expected, the other court officials became jealous and began to look for a way to pull Daniel down. They could find nothing in his character or work ethic to attack, so they chose to destroy him using two deceitful weapons: Daniel's odd religious practices and the king's ego. And on the surface, it worked like a charm.

The officials banded together and persuaded King Darius to proclaim an edict that no one in the kingdom could pray to any other deity except the king himself. The penalty for praying would be a visit to a den of hungry lions. This special act of allegiance was to last for thirty days. To the naïve Darius, it seemed like a wonderful patriotic idea when he heard it. But the officials knew Daniel would not break his practice of praying to his God, even for thirty days.

The stage was set, and the plot unfolded just as Daniel's enemies thought it would. Daniel learned of the edict, but continued to kneel and pray to his God three times a day, facing Jerusalem from his quiet room. He showed the same uncompromising courage he had when as a young man he refused to eat the unclean food from Nebuchadnezzar's table. And he showed the same defiance that his three friends had shown when they faced the Babylonian's fiery furnace.

He was caught in the act of praying and the king was notified right away. Darius saw through the trap, but it was too late. He could not spare Daniel from the lion's den because he would lose face with his court and perhaps his entire kingdom. Daniel's only hope was a direct intervention by God. And once again, the result is the stuff of Sunday School legend. God delivered Daniel from the mouths of the lions; and his wicked enemies were tossed to their deaths in his place.

King Darius was so impressed by the power of Daniel's God that he made a decree:

> *Then King Darius wrote to all the nations and peoples of every language in all the earth: "May you prosper greatly! I issue a decree that in every part of my kingdom people must fear and reverence the God of Daniel. For he is the living God and he endures forever; his kingdom will not be destroyed, his dominion will never end. He rescues and he saves; he performs signs and wonders in the heavens and on the earth. He has rescued Daniel from the power of the lions."*
>
> *So Daniel prospered during the reign of Darius and the reign of Cyrus the Persian. (Daniel 6:25-28)*

Daniel's courage proved to be a witness to the entire world of the power and faithfulness of the God of Israel.

Visions, Prayers and Answers

The book of Daniel takes a dramatic turn in its focus after chapter 6. This is because Daniel's life took a drastic turn. As a youth, he experienced upheaval in being exiled to Babylon. He then learned to thrive as a royal advisor and official. He was even able to identify and interpret others' dreams. But God brought another major turn in his life. He was to become God's prophet, and this was no easy job.

Let's quickly review Daniel's story up to this point. A group of young Hebrews were uprooted from their culture and thrust into a pagan society. They stood firm in their faith and experienced God's blessing because of their courage, tact and God-given natural ability. To borrow Jesus' words, Daniel and his friends were among wolves and were given wisdom to be shrewd as snakes but as innocent as doves. (Matthew 10:16) Because of their character and actions, people of other nations came to learn about the power of the One True God.

But starting in chapter 7, we read that Daniel began to have dreams of his own, and they perplexed him greatly. God gave him a series of visions over many years pointing to what was going to happen in the future. It was to be a long, perplexing period of time where Daniel had more questions than answers.

We can only imagine that the deepest desire of Daniel's heart was to see the people of Israel return to the Promised Land and reclaim Jerusalem as their own inheritance. In fact, it is quite possible that when Daniel prayed three times a day facing Jerusalem, this would have been a central part of his petition before God.

For whatever reason, God decided to make Daniel a prophet. Prophets in the Old Testament often had two roles: "forthtelling" and "foretelling." Prophets like Elijah generally told forth to the people of Israel what God wanted them to do – return to the covenant and put away false gods. Prophets like Isaiah not only proclaimed this same message, but were granted revelation to foretell what would happen in the future – especially prophesying the coming of the Messiah. Daniel's role of a prophet seemed to include a tremendous amount of "foretelling," or laying out what the future would hold.

In an apocalyptic style with many fantastic images and mysterious symbols, God revealed to Daniel the rising and falling of many kingdoms until the coming of God's eternal reign. Daniel's dreams in chapters 7 and 8 included violent winds, destructive horned beasts, the appearance of the Ancient of Days, one like a Son of Man, and even the angel Gabriel. As a result of all his visions, Daniel was perplexed and incapacitated for a time.

> *"I, Daniel, was troubled in spirit, and the visions that passed through my mind disturbed me. (Daniel 7:15)*

> *"I, Daniel, was deeply troubled by my thoughts, and my face turned pale, but I kept the matter to myself." (Daniel 7:28)*

> *I, Daniel, was worn out. I lay exhausted for several days. Then I got up and went about the king's business. I was appalled by the vision; it was beyond understanding. (Daniel 8:27)*

Being God's prophet was not always easy. Daniel had dreams and visions over a long period of time, during the reigns of Belshazzar King of Babylon, Darius the Mede, and Cyrus King of Persia. Seeing into the future can be dangerous business, and God chose to put Daniel through this. In the midst of all his confusion about what God had shown him, he turned to the Scriptures and to prayer to gain greater understanding.

In addition to being God's prophet, Daniel took on the role of intercessor for his entire nation. In chapter 9, we see him acting like a priest, confessing the sins of the people of Israel. He had been studying the words of the prophet Jeremiah and had come to understand that Jerusalem would lay in ruins for seventy years. (Jeremiah 25:11-12) This discovery drove him to prayer, while fasting and being dressed mournfully in sackcloth and ashes. The time was drawing near for his nation to be restored.

His beautiful prayer is recorded for us in Daniel chapter 9. Daniel called upon his great covenant-keeping God and confessed in great detail the sins of his people. They had rebelled against God; they had broken his commands and disregarded the proclamations of God's prophets. He went on to declare that his entire nation was covered with shame and disgrace because God had given them over to their enemies and cast them out of the Promised Land. Nevertheless, Daniel called upon God's mercy to forgive and restore His sinful people for the sake of God's own glory. Here is the conclusion of his priestly prayer:

"Now, our God, hear the prayers and petitions of your servant. For your sake, Lord, look with favor on your desolate sanctuary. Give ear, our God, and hear; open your eyes and see the desolation of the city that bears your Name. We do not make requests of you because we are righteous, but because of your great mercy. Lord, listen! Lord, forgive! Lord, hear and act! For your sake, my God, do not delay, because your city and your people bear your Name." (Daniel 9:17-19)

Daniel's prayer certainly got God's attention. He sent His angel Gabriel to give Daniel additional information, although most of this new data was just as cryptic as what he had previously received.

In chapter 10, we see that Daniel's visions continued; he saw a figure of a man like no other he had ever seen. And once again, he was terrified.

At that time I, Daniel, mourned for three weeks. I ate no choice food; no meat or wine touched my lips; and I used no lotions at all until the three weeks were over.

On the twenty-fourth day of the first month, as I was standing on the bank of the great river, the Tigris, I looked up and there before me was a man dressed in linen, with a belt of fine gold from Uphaz around his waist. His body was like topaz, his face like lightning, his eyes like flaming torches, his arms and legs like the gleam of burnished bronze, and his voice like the sound of a multitude.

I, Daniel, was the only one who saw the vision; those who were with me did not see it, but such terror overwhelmed them that they fled and hid themselves. So I was left alone, gazing at this great vision; I had no strength left, my face turned deathly pale and I was helpless. Then I heard him speaking, and as I listened to him, I fell into a deep sleep, my face to the ground. (Daniel 10:2-9)

Why was Daniel the recipient of these fantastic visions? The answer is, in part, he asked for it. The glowing man told him:

"Do not be afraid, Daniel. Since the first day that you set your mind to gain understanding and to humble yourself before your God, your words were heard, and I have come in response to them." (Daniel 10:12)

Daniel was a man who sought God and prayed earnestly and humbly for answers. He received these words from God because he asked.

It is not my purpose to interpret the visions of Daniel; that is beyond the scope of this book. Suffice it to say Daniel was given a lengthy look into the future history of this world and the end times. God delivered this message to him because he asked. God used Daniel's visions to shed light on His plan in history that all of us may ponder and benefit from.

I am sure Daniel still had questions at the end of his life. Many of the visions he saw he had not understood. He asked one of the angelic figures in his vision to help him understand all that had been revealed to him. The answer he got may have been a bit disappointing.

I heard, but I did not understand. So I asked, "My lord, what will the outcome of all this be?"

He replied, "Go your way, Daniel, because the words are rolled up and sealed until the time of the end. Many will be purified, made spotless and refined, but the wicked will continue to be wicked. None of the wicked will understand, but those who are wise will understand." (Daniel 12:8-10)

He would not live to see the culmination of God's plan, nor did he get to return to his beloved Jerusalem. The concluding words of this book are spoken to him by the glowing figure of a man:

"As for you, go your way till the end. You will rest, and then at the end of the days you will rise to receive your allotted inheritance." (Daniel 12:13)

Like Moses, Daniel did not live to see God's promises fulfilled. He was simply told to "go his way." His life ended with several loose ends. And like all other human stories, this is because his life was not merely about him.

The End of the Line

What lessons can we take away from the life of Daniel? There are many!

- Like Daniel, we are immersed in a culture that openly opposes the One True God. Daniel and his friends succeeded in their lives by exhibiting courage, integrity and tact. We too should look at perilous times as courageous opportunities. Refusing to eat unclean food, declining to bow down to a king who called himself a god, ignoring the edict to stop praying to God, and facing a den of lions were all acts of remarkable courage. God honored such courage, and continued to exalt Daniel and his friends in their pagan culture. Courage, integrity and tact on the part of believers can be a great witness through which the nations come to hear of the power of God.

- Like Joseph years earlier, Daniel "bloomed where he was planted." We never read of him complaining or wishing he were someplace else. He was also subjected to hateful bigotry and treachery by others in power. Godly people will face evil opposition; we are not promised an easy road.

- Daniel was a man of prayer – he not only prayed for himself but for his entire nation. Daniel's patience was remarkable as he waited for God to allow his people to return from exile to the Promised Land. He prayed for that day, and God revealed to him many great mysteries concerning the future and God's plan for the world. Perhaps we too can take on the prayerful task of praying for our world and for God's kingdom to come.

- Part of the crooked paths in Daniel's life involved the many visions of the future he received. Becoming God's prophet meant a completely new direction in his life which he did not expect. All those visions did not yank him around physically, but they truly did emotionally and mentally. Why did God upset him so? In part, for our benefit. Daniel's prophecies remain for us today, and they point to the complete sovereignty of God, the coming of Christ and the establishment of His eternal kingdom.

- Nothing is said negatively about Daniel, which is truly remarkable. But as Jesus said in Luke 12:48, *"From everyone who has been given much, much will be demanded; and from the one who has been entrusted with much, much more will be asked."* God rocked Daniel's world by giving him a prophetic ministry he did not ask for or expect in his wildest dreams. He was able to understand certain aspects of his visions – like the coming of the future empires of the Medes, Persians, Greeks and Romans. But much of the information was so incredible it literally made him ill. He was faithful in delivering the cryptic information for us to ponder. When God calls us to unexpected tasks we cannot completely understand, we should be faithful and follow God's leading. Only God knows and understands all of the future, because He is completely sovereign over it all.

Daniel's life did not have what we might call "closure." At the end of his life he had unfulfilled dreams. He received great visions, but did not live to see them come to pass. Complete closure rarely comes in this life for any of us. It is good to remember that our lives are not ultimately about us, but about the plans and purposes of God.

Questions for Reflection and Discussion

1. Daniel was quite literally a human "spoil of war." Are there any modern-day equivalents to such an experience?

2. Daniel and his friends resolved to stand up against some strict rules of an oppressive government. How did God honor this? Are there instances in our world today where God's people are called to act as Daniel did?

3. Which of Daniel's many positive character traits do you most admire (e.g., courage, tact, moral integrity)?

4. Daniel successfully walked the line between "being in the world but not of it." What were the keys to his success, and how might we emulate him?

5. Describe Daniel's prayer life. How did he pray and what did he pray for? Are there lessons here for you?

6. Daniel took on several jobs simultaneously during his life: faithful government worker, priest and intercessor for his people, and prophet foretelling the future. What life tasks are you trying to accomplish simultaneously? What are your coping strategies when called to accomplish difficult tasks?

7. Daniel was overwhelmed by the visions God showed him concerning the future. As a result, he often had more questions than answers. How do you try to deal with unanswered questions in your relationship to God?

Switchbacks

10

A Path to Ponder: MARY

"I am the Lord's servant," Mary answered. "May your word to me be fulfilled." (Luke 1:38)

In the New Testament, the life of Mary is often tied inextricably to the life of her son. But it is worth taking a closer look at her personal journey to gain insight into how God might work in our own lives.

Surprising News

In the gospel accounts, we first meet Mary when she was a young girl in Nazareth – possibly as young as twelve or fourteen. She was betrothed to an older man, the carpenter Joseph. Luke's gospel account is the most complete of the four gospels as it relates to Mary. We learn she was a virgin, and her fiancé was a descendant of David. We also learn early on that these two people were devout, God-fearing Jews, seeking to obey the Lord in all things. And soon, remarkable things were going to happen in their lives.

In the first chapter of Luke, God initiated the conversation and the events by sending the angel Gabriel to Mary. Mary was going about her business when God broke into her life in a remarkable way.

> *The angel went to her and said, "Greetings, you who are highly favored! The Lord is with you." Mary was greatly troubled at his words and wondered what kind of greeting this might be. But the angel said to her, "Do not be afraid, Mary; you have found favor with God. You will conceive and give birth to a son, and you are to call him Jesus. He will be great and will be called the Son of the Most High. The Lord God will give him the throne of his father David, and he will reign over Jacob's descendants forever; his kingdom will never end." (Luke 1:28-33)*

We call this familiar but life-changing event "The Annunciation." But imagine how this news must have been first received by Mary. To say the least, it was a lot to absorb in a short amount of time. She experienced fear, while having to come to understand that she was to become pregnant. And her son, who was to be named Jesus, would be an eternal king – the Messiah. Her initial response is understandable:

"How will this be," Mary asked the angel, "since I am a virgin?" (Luke 1:34)

It was an honest question – and one Mary probably would ask again and again throughout her life as it related to Jesus' ministry: "How can this be?" At this point, Mary understood that she was to become pregnant before having relations with her betrothed husband, Joseph. God graciously gave her more information.

The angel answered, "The Holy Spirit will come on you, and the power of the Most High will overshadow you. So the holy one to be born will be called the Son of God. Even Elizabeth your relative is going to have a child in her old age, and she who was said to be unable to conceive is in her sixth month. For no word from God will ever fail." (Luke 1:35-37)

She was to become the mother of the Son of God! The Holy Spirit would work a miracle inside her womb. And as further proof this would happen, Gabriel told her that Mary's elderly relative Elizabeth, who had been barren for many years, was six months pregnant. It appears that God was working two miracles in close succession. Much to her credit, Mary believed all the angel told her and surrendered to the Lord's plan:

"I am the Lord's servant," Mary answered. "May your word to me be fulfilled." Then the angel left her. (Luke 1:38)

This could be the biggest twist and turn in the Bible. Imagine how other women might have reacted to this information. What an obedient response, given what the consequences might be! Mary's response to the angel's message would become her life's motto. She was about to embark on a lifelong adventure filled with crooked paths.

After receiving the message, Mary hurried to Elizabeth, and Gabriel's message was confirmed. Elizabeth was indeed about to give birth. How gracious of God to give Mary such confirmation! Both women seemed to have been aware of what God was doing, and were filled with the Holy Spirit.

When Elizabeth heard Mary's greeting, the baby leaped in her womb, and Elizabeth was filled with the Holy Spirit. In a loud voice she exclaimed: "Blessed are you among women, and blessed is the child you will bear! But why am I so favored, that the mother of my Lord should come to me? As soon as the sound of your greeting reached my ears, the baby in my womb leaped for joy. Blessed is she who has believed that the Lord would fulfill his promises to her!" (Luke 1:41-45)

Mary's response to Elizabeth's greeting has come to be known as "The Magnificat." Mary praised the Lord from the deepest parts of her being, and exclaimed that He had shown favor to the humblest of His servants.

And Mary said:

"My soul glorifies the Lord and my spirit rejoices in God my Savior, for he has been mindful of the humble state of his servant. From now on all generations will call me blessed, for the Mighty One has done great things for me – holy is his name. His mercy extends to those who fear him, from generation to generation. He has performed mighty deeds with his arm; he has scattered those who are proud in their inmost thoughts. He has brought down rulers from their thrones but has lifted up the humble. He has filled the hungry with good things but has sent the rich away empty. He has helped his servant Israel, remembering to be merciful to Abraham and his descendants forever, just as he promised our ancestors." (Luke 1:46-55)

It was a time of great expectations for Mary, and indeed for all of Israel. God was moving and His Messiah was coming. But hidden in the words of Mary's song were her preconceived notions of how God's deliverance would come. She spoke of the proud being scattered, of thrones being brought down, and the rich oppressors being sent away empty. Might she have expected her son, the Messiah, to become a political ruler and a deliverer of Israel from Roman tyranny? Most Jews were hoping for the Messiah to do this and prayed for it to happen. We can only speculate. But how God actually moved would take some unseen turns, perhaps causing Mary to have more questions than answers along the way.

What a Way to Start a Marriage!

In Matthew's gospel, we read of how Joseph reacted to the news brought to him by Mary. His fiancé is pregnant by the Holy Spirit. This must have been a tough pill to swallow.

This is how the birth of Jesus the Messiah came about: His mother Mary was pledged to be married to Joseph, but before they came together, she was found to be pregnant through the Holy Spirit. Because Joseph her husband was faithful to the law, and yet did not want to expose her to public disgrace, he had in mind to divorce her quietly. But after he had considered this, an angel of the Lord appeared to him in a dream and said, "Joseph son of David, do not be afraid to take Mary home as your wife, because what is conceived in her is from the Holy Spirit. She will give birth to a son, and you are to give him the name Jesus, because he will save his people from their sins." (Mt.1:18-21)

Imagine the social stigma and scandal this pregnancy caused. Over time, it became impossible to hide the fact the unmarried Mary was with child. In the small village of Nazareth, there were probably lots of loose tongues and rolling eyes. The public shame and shunning that may have taken place would have been understandable in that culture.

And as if things were not uncomfortable enough, the Roman government was about to make things even more complicated. Caesar Augustus decreed a census had to be taken. This meant everyone had to return to their native town to be registered. Joseph, being a descendant of David, had to travel with Mary to Bethlehem.

Let's stop for a moment and reflect upon what has happened in Mary and Joseph's lives in the past few months. What began as a simple engagement and plans for a humble life together had turned into a major crisis on many levels. Mary's pregnancy, social scandal, government upheaval and unplanned travel have created a chaotic situation. Since Gabriel's announcement to Mary, their expectations and aspirations have been turned upside down. If I were Mary or Joseph, this series of events might have shaken my faith in God and filled me with fear. *What was God doing here?* And yet, this new couple were right in the center of God's will for their lives, even though they might not have felt that way.

We know the Christmas story, and we often romanticize it. But it was far from a pleasant scene. Mary and Joseph traveled to Bethlehem, Mary was "great with child," so it probably was a very uncomfortable journey. There was no room in the inn, so they took refuge in a lowly cattle shed where Jesus was born. As one Christmas carol puts it, Jesus was born "betwixt an ox and a silly poor ass." Mary's firstborn son was placed in a feeding trough and wrapped in rags. This couple had next to nothing to start out life together – except each other and God.

The new parents had to wonder what would happen next. The special child had been born and was now in their care. Where were they to go from here?

It was at this time that God brought some much-needed confirmation of His plan into their lives. A group of shepherds appeared and told of angels announcing to them the birth of the Messiah. Mary and Joseph had to view the arrival of the shepherds to the manger as an encouragement from God. We read these mysterious yet wonderful words in Luke 2:19: *"But Mary treasured up all these things and pondered them in her heart."*

God soon provided additional confirmation to Mary and Joseph. When it came time to circumcise and dedicate their firstborn son to God in the temple, two elderly Jews – one male and one female – made remarkable pronouncements about the baby Jesus.

First, an old man pronounced in a prophetic way that this child born to Mary would be the Messiah:

Now there was a man in Jerusalem called Simeon, who was righteous and devout. He was waiting for the consolation of Israel, and the Holy Spirit was on him. It had been revealed to him by the Holy Spirit that he would not die before he had seen the Lord's Messiah. Moved by the Spirit, he went into the temple courts. When the parents brought in the child Jesus to do for him what the custom of the Law required, Simeon took him in his arms and praised God, saying:

"Sovereign Lord, as you have promised, you may now dismiss your servant in peace. For my eyes have seen your salvation, which you have prepared in the sight of all nations: a light for revelation to the Gentiles, and the glory of your people Israel."

The child's father and mother marveled at what was said about him. Then Simeon blessed them and said to Mary, his mother:

"This child is destined to cause the falling and rising of many in Israel, and to be a sign that will be spoken against, so that the thoughts of many hearts will be revealed. And a sword will pierce your own soul too." (Luke 2:25-35)

And as if to confirm the testimony of one witness with that of another, an old woman echoed Simeon's pronouncement.

There was also a prophet, Anna, the daughter of Penuel, of the tribe of Asher. She was very old; she had lived with her husband seven years after her marriage, and then was a widow until she was eighty-four. She never left the temple but worshiped night and day, fasting and praying. Coming up to them at that very moment, she gave thanks to God and spoke about the child to all who were looking forward to the redemption of Jerusalem. (Luke 2:36-38)

Once again, this was a time of potential information overload for Mary. There was so much to figure out and try to put together! What were Mary and Joseph to do to accomplish God's will?

Sometime later after these events, we read in Matthew's gospel that more special visitors greeted Jesus, Mary and Joseph. This time, it was wise men from the East. The visitation of the Magi provided additional confirmation of God's plan, along with valuable royal gifts. But the most precious gift they gave was one of life-saving information. King Herod was going to try to kill their infant son, because he had learned that a potential Messiah had been born in Bethlehem. So, Mary, Joseph and their child fled to Egypt. They were uprooted once again, and lived as refugees in a strange land for quite a while.

If I were Mary, I might have had a meltdown at this point. God had promised that her son would be the King of Kings and Lord of Lords – ruler of Israel. And now she was running for her life to Egypt. What had Egypt to do with God's promises to her?

And what is it about *Egypt*, anyway? Remember Abram had to flee to Egypt because of an ancient famine in Canaan? And Joseph was taken to Egypt early in his own zig-zag life. God seems to like to send His people to this foreign land as part of his plan. Might you have had an "Egypt experience" in your life? Why does God's plan have to be so hard? Why so many twists and turns? As one of my former pastors used to say, it seems that God likes to move us "from security to trust."

Well, back to Mary's story.

Raising an Adolescent

Once the wicked King Herod was dead, the danger had passed. Mary, her husband, and the boy Jesus returned to Nazareth and life became routine – at least for a while. Luke summarizes Jesus' early years with a simple sentence:

> *And the child grew and became strong; he was filled with wisdom, and the grace of God was on him. (Luke 2:40)*

A "normal" life began to unfold for Mary. We read in the gospel accounts that she had other children with Joseph – brothers and sisters along with their oldest son (Mark 6:3; Mt. 13:55-56). Jesus seemed to fit into life in Nazareth, and grew up like any other child. At least until one Passover year when the boy was twelve.

Mary and Joseph obviously knew their son was special, but at times they might have forgotten just how special. One Passover, while returning from Jerusalem, they misplaced the young Jesus for four days. Can you imagine being a parent and losing your child for four days? They thought he was returning from Jerusalem to Nazareth with their large entourage, but after one day into the return journey, they realized Jesus was not with them. They went back to Jerusalem and search frantically for him for three days. Might the conversation included some comment like this? *"Oh great, we have lost the Son of God and he's not even a teenager yet."*

I wonder where they looked? They must have searched every nook and cranny of the city, until they tried the temple courts, where they found him sitting with the teachers of the law listening to them and asking questions. We read in Luke's gospel:

Everyone who heard him was amazed at his understanding and his answers. When his parents saw him, they were astonished. His mother said to him, "Son, why have you treated us like this? Your father and I have been anxiously searching for you."

"Why were you searching for me?" he asked. "Didn't you know I had to be in my Father's house?" But they did not understand what he was saying to them. Then he went down to Nazareth with them and was obedient to them. But his mother treasured all these things in her heart. (Luke 2:47-51)

Jesus answered Mary's question with questions of his own. At the young age of twelve, He was already a good rabbi! Mary was reminded once again that Jesus' life was going to be different and full of surprises – for her as well as for the entire world. How could anyone anticipate what was to unfold in the life of her son?

The Start of Jesus' Ministry

The next time we encounter Mary is at a wedding in the tiny town of Cana. A lot of life had passed by. At this point, it is quite possible Jesus was in his thirties and had started his ministry – he had a few disciples around him already. We can also assume Mary had already lost her husband, Joseph. Her oldest son was very precious to her.

A crisis arose at a wedding feast – the host family had run out of wine. This was a major social embarrassment in this culture, and Mary decided to press Jesus into doing something about it. He was a man now, so if he were to start his ministry as the Messiah, it may be time to get going. She obviously believed that Jesus could do something to solve the problem, and yet her son seemed reluctant to act at first.

When the wine was gone, Jesus' mother said to him, "They have no more wine."

> *"Woman, why do you involve me?" Jesus replied. "My hour has not yet come."*
>
> *His mother said to the servants, "Do whatever he tells you." Nearby stood six stone water jars, the kind used by the Jews for ceremonial washing, each holding from twenty to thirty gallons.*
>
> *Jesus said to the servants, "Fill the jars with water"; so they filled them to the brim. Then he told them, "Now draw some out and take it to the master of the banquet." They did so, and the master of the banquet tasted the water that had been turned into wine. He did not realize where it had come from, though the servants who had drawn the water knew.*
>
> *Then he called the bridegroom aside and said, "Everyone brings out the choice wine first and then the cheaper wine after the guests have had too much to drink; but you have saved the best till now." What Jesus did here in Cana of Galilee was the first of the signs through which he revealed his glory; and his disciples believed in him. (John 2:3-11)*

At this point, Jesus fulfilled Mary's expectations and acted in a way she thought the Messiah should act. He had turned water into wine. But it seemed as Jesus' ministry unfolded, Mary was to have growing questions about how Jesus was proceeding with his life's work. Like mothers everywhere, she had to deal with losing control over the life of her child. He was an adult now and was making his own decisions. She was becoming more of a spectator than a participant.

Even early in Jesus' ministry, he was ruffling the feathers of the Jewish leaders. Opposition was mounting – both religious and political. Elizabeth's son John the Baptist had been arrested and beheaded. These had to be fearful events for Mary to ponder. Her son was in danger, and He needed to be careful how He acted and reacted to others.

Like any mother, she certainly had opinions and advice to give to her son. Mary may have been having serious questions with the way Jesus was running things. This must have been a major crisis point in Mary's life! Then we read a remarkable passage from Mark 3:20-21.

> *Then Jesus entered a house, and again a crowd gathered, so that he and his disciples were not even able to eat. When his family heard about this, they went to take charge of him, for they said, "He is out of his mind."*

Jesus' mother and brothers were far from convinced that Jesus was on the right track. In modern terms, Jesus' family tried to stage an intervention. This had to be a tough time for Mary. What was going to happen to all the promises she received from Gabriel, the angel of the Lord? And what was going to happen to all the words of confirmation she had received from the shepherds, Simeon, Anna and the Magi so long ago? It all seemed to be going in a strange direction, and this had to be terribly confusing.

And to make things worse, Jesus seemed to snub his mother and brothers publicly.

Jesus' mother and brothers arrived. Standing outside, they sent someone in to call him. A crowd was sitting around him, and they told him, "Your mother and brothers are outside looking for you."

"Who are my mother and my brothers?" he asked.

Then he looked at those seated in a circle around him and said, "Here are my mother and my brothers! Whoever does God's will is my brother and sister and mother." (Mark 3:31-34)

Jesus let Mary know he was in control of his life and ministry, not her. This is a tough lesson for any parent to learn. She would have to sit and watch events unfold and continue to ponder them in her heart.

Shortly after this encounter, Jesus met strong unbelief in his home town of Nazareth – from members of his own family. Jesus' response to this was strong and direct:

"Only in his home town, among his relatives and in his own house is a prophet without honor." He could not do any miracles there, except lay hands on a few sick people and heal them. And he was amazed at their lack of faith. (Mark 6:4-6)

It may seem shocking to hear of unbelief within the "Holy Family" itself, but it is not surprising, really. Would we have reacted any differently? And ultimately, Jesus did not condemn them for it.

The Culmination of Jesus' Ministry

From here on, perhaps Mary had to passively watch Jesus move towards the cross, supporting her son as best she could. Maybe the words of Simeon rang true in her ears from so many years earlier: *"And a sword will pierce your own soul too."* (Luke 2:35)

What an emotional roller coaster she must have been on! Watching Jesus' miracles and the immense popularity with the crowds, witnessing the mounting opposition of the

Jewish elite, observing the Triumphal Entry on Palm Sunday, and a week later, hearing the crowds shout "Crucify him! Crucify him!" Where were the straight paths God should be providing?

We read in John's gospel that Mary was there at the foot of the cross when Jesus died.

> *Near the cross of Jesus stood his mother, his mother's sister, Mary the wife of Clopas, and Mary Magdalene. When Jesus saw his mother there, and the disciple whom he loved standing nearby, he said to her, "Woman, here is your son," and to the disciple, "Here is your mother." From that time on, this disciple took her into his home. (John 19:25-27)*

Mary was given into John's care by her dying son, and she remained in his care the rest of her life. After Jesus' death, no doubt she suffered unbearable grief. I am drawn to the immortal image created in the sculpture by Michelangelo – *The Pieta*, where Mary is holding the body of her dead son. And after this grief came Jesus' resurrection, and unspeakable joy. God gave Mary many confirmations of His promises throughout her life. The greatest of these was her son's resurrection from the dead. God's plan of salvation finally made sense after Jesus' resurrection and ascension. Easter Sunday for Mary was the greatest confirmation she ever received.

Many of the mysteries of her life began to make sense – but only in hindsight. Like Joseph long ago in Egypt, Mary had the rare privilege of seeing the purpose in God's winding road for her life. The Messiah would have to suffer and die and rise again according to the Scriptures.

After Jesus ascended to heaven, we read that Mary was with the disciples in the earliest days of the church, along with her other sons.

> *Then the apostles returned to Jerusalem from the hill called the Mount of Olives, a Sabbath day's walk from the city. When they arrived, they went upstairs to the room where they were staying. Those present were Peter, John, James and Andrew; Philip and Thomas, Bartholomew and Matthew; James son of Alphaeus and Simon the Zealot, and Judas son of James. They all joined together constantly in prayer, along with the women and Mary the mother of Jesus, and with his brothers. (Acts 1:12-14)*

The real adventure was just beginning for Mary and the early church. We know she was present at Pentecost (Acts 2:1-4) and was baptized with the Holy Spirit.

Switchbacks

We do not know anything about Mary after her experience at Pentecost. But wouldn't we love to know? The Bible is silent on this subject. This is a reminder that Mary's story is not the central one of Scripture, but God's story and purposes are. Tradition tells us Mary may have traveled with John to Ephesus, where she would have witnessed the growth of the fledgling church under Timothy's leadership. It is also possible she stayed in Jerusalem under John's indirect care.

The End of the Line

There are strong lessons we can take away from this wonderful life of a servant of the Lord.

- Time and again God would send gracious confirmation that He was indeed in control in Mary's life. Elizabeth's pregnancy, Joseph's belief and support, the shepherds arrival at the manger, Simeon and Anna at the temple, the Wise Men's visit – all confirmations that God was in control and His promises could be counted upon. And the biggest confirmation occurred Easter Sunday morning. When we walk in obedience to Him, God gives us confirmation, too, if we look for it.

- Like Mary, we have expectations on how God will work in our lives and in the lives of these we love. None of us come to God and His plan as a blank slate, or *tabula rasa*. We have to learn to be flexible and receptive to God's ways. Mary is a shining example of this for us. Like so many others who seek to walk with God, Mary's life was full of twists and turns and "switchbacks." Like all the Jews of her day, she had expectations as to how the Messiah would come and establish His Kingdom on earth. When Jesus did not meet these expectations, she experienced uncertainty, confusion and turmoil. There came a crisis point where members of her family believed Jesus might have been out of his mind! And why did a sword have to pierce her heart? She watched her son die, but then she saw the culmination and fulfillment of God's plan of salvation. And Mary had to come to a personal, saving faith in the Son of God like everyone else. We will come to places of turmoil and crisis as well, and this is where God can meet us in remarkable ways.

- Sometimes we find ourselves in very difficult situations, and yet we are right smack dab in the center of God's will for our lives. In the midst of the most fearful and uncertain times in her life, Mary was in the center of God's will. Whether she was fearing social ostracization as a pregnant young girl, penniless and pregnant in Bethlehem, fleeing to Egypt from Herod, frantically searching for her lost 12-year old in Jerusalem, losing her husband, wrestling with Jesus' hard teachings, or watching Him suffer and die on the cross, there was a surrender and acceptance that permeated all her actions. She was an extremely flexible and adaptable woman! Can we learn to be this adaptable? Yes, by the grace of God.

When we are tempted to call out – *"God, are you out of your mind? Why is this happening to me?"* Think about the life of Mary – and remember the faithfulness of God.

In the end, all God promised Mary did come true – but there were few straight paths.

My wife's grandmother was a godly woman whose testimony caused her entire family to come to know the Lord Jesus as Savior. She often described her own topsy-turvy life as being like a cork floating on the ocean, going where God's current led her.

This is not a bad way to live.

"I am the Lord's servant," Mary answered. "May your word to me be fulfilled."
(Luke 1:38)

Questions for Reflection and Discussion

1. Mary had many difficult things to endure during her life, including fear of rejection, social scandal, uprootedness, and unmet expectations. Yet God was in control at every step. How did she respond to these trials, and what lessons are there for you in her story?

2. Throughout her life, God graciously provided confirmation to Mary that He was indeed faithful. We see this in the circumstances of Elizabeth's pregnancy in old age, the appearance of the shepherds and wise men, the pronouncements of Simeon and Anna, and ultimately, Jesus' resurrection. Has God provided moments of confirmation that He is at work in your life?

3. When Mary and Joseph had to flee from Herod to Egypt, what do you think were the emotions they had to deal with? Has God ever presented you with an "Egypt" experience?

4. Mary had preconceptions about how her son's ministry would unfold. How did God lead her to truly understand His divine plan? Are there preconceived notions that you hold about how God will work in your life that the Lord may want you to change?

5. Like every mother, Mary had to learn to let go of controlling her child's life. Reflect upon how difficult this often is for parents to do. Why do you think this is the case?

David Rox

Switchbacks

11

Coming to the Crossroads: PAUL

"I was not disobedient to the vision from heaven." (Acts 26:19)

What a man Paul must have been! What a life he lived! Next to the Lord Jesus himself, there is no one who dominates the pages of the New Testament more than the Apostle Paul.

As we look at his life, we see one major turn in direction and many twists after that. Who could have predicted how this one life would influence the course of all history?

The Bigoted Jewish Pharisee

Saul (as he was first named) was born in Tarsus, an important Roman city in Cilicia on the coast of the Mediterranean Sea, not far from Antioch. Much of what we know about his background we learn from his own description in his letters and in the book of Acts. He was a Jew and a Roman citizen by birth, and was raised as a Pharisee in the strictest of schools, tutored by the great rabbi Gamaliel in Jerusalem. We learn later in Acts 18 that he was by trade a tentmaker, or tradesman in leather goods. Listen to his own words as he described his background.

> *I studied under Gamaliel and was thoroughly trained in the law of our ancestors. I was just as zealous for God as any of you are today. (Acts 22:3)*

> *The Jewish people all know the way I have lived ever since I was a child, from the beginning of my life in my own country, and also in Jerusalem. They have known me for a long time and can testify, if they are willing, that I conformed to the strictest sect of our religion, living as a Pharisee. (Acts 26:4-5)*

> *If someone else thinks they have reasons to put confidence in the flesh, I have more: circumcised on the eighth day, of the people of Israel, of the tribe of Benjamin, a Hebrew of Hebrews; in regard to the law, a Pharisee; as for zeal,*

persecuting the church; as for righteousness based on the law, faultless. (Philippians 3:4-6)

As a young man, Saul was confronted with the message of the Gospel and the claims of those followers of Jesus Christ. He viewed this new message as blasphemy – as an affront to the God of Israel. Among Pharisees, this was certainly the majority opinion. The Messiah would not come to die for his people. Jesus had claimed to be the Son of God, and this was too much to believe for most Jews. Jesus had been nailed to a Roman cross, and that was to be the end of it. When the disciples of Christ continued to teach and perform miracles in the name of Jesus of Nazareth, the Jewish leaders ordered them to stop teaching in this name. Peter and the other disciples bravely refused. Ironically, one voice warned the Sanhedrin to tread cautiously in dealing with this new sect. It was Saul's old teacher, Gamaliel.

But a Pharisee named Gamaliel, a teacher of the law, who was honored by all the people, stood up in the Sanhedrin and ordered that the men be put outside for a little while. Then he addressed the Sanhedrin: "Men of Israel, consider carefully what you intend to do to these men. Some time ago Theudas appeared, claiming to be somebody, and about four hundred men rallied to him. He was killed, all his followers were dispersed, and it all came to nothing. After him, Judas the Galilean appeared in the days of the census and led a band of people in revolt. He too was killed, and all his followers were scattered. Therefore, in the present case I advise you: Leave these men alone! Let them go! For if their purpose or activity is of human origin, it will fail. But if it is from God, you will not be able to stop these men; you will only find yourselves fighting against God. (Acts 5:33-39)

It seems Gamaliel's advice fell on deaf ears – especially when it came to his former pupil, Saul.

Saul was no mere bystander when he encountered the Christian message. He got involved. This shows us a lot about his personality – Saul of Tarsus was a man of action! His passion was to wipe out Christianity and purge it from Israel. We read in the book of Acts about the death of the deacon Stephen; while the martyr was being stoned, the Jews laid their cloaks at the feet of a young man named Saul. While this did not necessarily mean Saul was in charge of the execution, it did mean he was there, giving full approval to Stephen's death. (Acts 8:1)

After the death of Stephen, Saul went into action to show his zeal for his Jewish faith. He was convinced that Christianity was the biggest threat to the religion of his fathers,

Switchbacks

and he set out to make a mark for himself. All Christians were targets of his righteous indignation. The Greek words used to describe Saul's actions are also used frequently to describe the rage seen in wild animals.

> *Saul began to destroy the church. Going from house to house, he dragged off both men and women and put them in prison. (Acts 8:3)*

In Saul's mind, he was on a mission from God. He went as far to pursue Christians well beyond the confines of Jerusalem all the way to Damascus. He even secured letters from the High Priest in Jerusalem to make his actions official and completely legitimate.

Saul's rage and zeal knew no bounds. In modern day language, Saul was a domestic terrorist to the Christians of his day. If you were a first-century Christian, Saul was out to get you.

The Damascus Road

If I were God, here is a place I would have created a straight, simple path. Saul was a man who was destroying God's church. He was on the road to Damascus to continue his butchery. Why not just hit him with a bolt of lightning and end his life? After all, there was precedent for such actions by God. There are several instances in the Old and New Testaments where God destroyed opposition. When insolent men opposed Moses, the Lord inflicted plagues or even opened the earth to swallow some of them up. (Numbers 16:31) Earlier in the book of Acts, in chapter 5, the deceitful Christians Ananias and Sapphira were struck down instantly for lying to the Holy Spirit. And later in the same book, the wicked King Herod Agrippa was eaten with worms and died when he failed to give glory to God. (Acts 12:23)

God would have been well within His divine right to destroy Saul of Tarsus on the spot. But He had other plans. Saul was stopped in his tracks by a blinding light on the road to Damascus.

> *As he neared Damascus on his journey, suddenly a light from heaven flashed around him. He fell to the ground and heard a voice say to him, "Saul, Saul, why do you persecute me?"*
>
> *"Who are you, Lord?" Saul asked.*
>
> *"I am Jesus, whom you are persecuting," he replied. "Now get up and go into the city, and you will be told what you must do."*

> *The men traveling with Saul stood there speechless; they heard the sound but did not see anyone. Saul got up from the ground, but when he opened his eyes he could see nothing. So they led him by the hand into Damascus. For three days he was blind, and did not eat or drink anything. (Acts 9:3-9)*

As Paul would tell Timothy many years later:

> *I thank Christ Jesus our Lord, who has given me strength, that he considered me faithful, appointing me to his service. Even though I was once a blasphemer and a persecutor and a violent man, I was shown mercy because I acted in ignorance and unbelief. The grace of our Lord was poured out on me abundantly, along with the faith and the love that are in Christ Jesus. Here is a trustworthy saying that deserves full acceptance: Christ Jesus came into the world to save sinners—of whom I am the worst. But for that very reason I was shown mercy so that in me, the worst of sinners, Christ Jesus might display his immense patience as an example for those who would believe in him and receive eternal life. Now to the King eternal, immortal, invisible, the only God, be honor and glory for ever and ever. Amen. (I Timothy 1:12-17)*

Imagine the shock Saul experienced when he learned it was Jesus speaking to him. Talk about a paradigm shift! Saul's entire way of viewing the God he worshipped and his life's work were thrown into confusion. The following three days had to be the longest and most excruciating days of the young man's life. He had to grapple with the truth that Jesus Christ *was* the Son of God. This proud, confident and zealous Pharisee was laid low by the crucified and risen Messiah, and all he could do was repent, fast and pray.

A reluctant but obedient Christ-follower named Ananias was ordered by Jesus to go to Saul and give him hope and direction. Ananias is one of the great unsung heroes of the Bible. It took great courage to go to Saul, given his well-known reputation. Yet, he assured Saul of forgiveness and acceptance.

> *Placing his hands on Saul, he said, "Brother Saul, the Lord – Jesus, who appeared to you on the road as you were coming here – has sent me so that you may see again and be filled with the Holy Spirit." Immediately, something like scales fell from Saul's eyes, and he could see again. He got up and was baptized, and after taking some food, he regained his strength. (Acts 3:17-19)*

Switchbacks

While lying in a room on Straight Street in Damascus, Saul experienced new life in Christ solely by the grace of God. What was to become of him now? We see an early glimpse of God's plan for Saul in the message Christ shared with Ananias, when he was ordered to visit Saul:

> *"This man is my chosen instrument to proclaim my name to the Gentiles and their kings and to the people of Israel. I will show him how much he must suffer for my name." (Acts 9:15-16)*

So, Saul was given a new purpose for his life – one completely unexpected for a bigoted Jewish Pharisee. You talk about zig-zags! He was to be Christ's chosen man to proclaim the Christian gospel to the Gentiles. *To the Gentiles?* Could there have been a more bizarre choice to take on this task? And Saul, who inflicted so much suffering on many Christians was to suffer greatly for Christ himself in his new occupation.

Although the purpose of Saul's life had completely changed, his activist personality did not. And serious danger became his early companion.

> *Saul spent several days with the disciples in Damascus. At once he began to preach in the synagogues that Jesus is the Son of God. All those who heard him were astonished and asked, "Isn't he the man who raised havoc in Jerusalem among those who call on this name? And hasn't he come here to take them as prisoners to the chief priests?" Yet Saul grew more and more powerful and baffled the Jews living in Damascus by proving that Jesus is the Messiah.*
>
> *After many days had gone by, there was a conspiracy among the Jews to kill him, but Saul learned of their plan. Day and night they kept close watch on the city gates in order to kill him. But his followers took him by night and lowered him in a basket through an opening in the wall. (Acts 9:19-25)*

Some heroes have no names – like the men who lowered the basket with Paul in it! This was only the first of many life-threatening situations for Saul of Tarsus. He was an activist and an agitator. It was part of his personality before meeting Jesus, and the Lord used this unique personality trait after his Damascus road experience. If you were a Christian in the first century who loved peace and quiet, Saul (now to be known as Paul) was not a person you would necessarily want around.

I notice that Saul is a Hebrew name and Paul is a Gentile name. When Saul came to realize that God had called him to minister to the Gentiles, I wonder if he chose his

Gentile name over his Hebrew one. Did he start calling himself Paul? At any rate, he accepted the role God gave him.

Time in Arabia

We read in Paul's letter to the church in Galatia about his early experience as a Christian.

> *I want you to know, brothers and sisters, that the gospel I preached is not of human origin. I did not receive it from any man, nor was I taught it; rather, I received it by revelation from Jesus Christ. For you have heard of my previous way of life in Judaism, how intensely I persecuted the church of God and tried to destroy it. I was advancing in Judaism beyond many of my own age among my people and was extremely zealous for the traditions of my fathers. But when God, who set me apart from my mother's womb and called me by his grace, was pleased to reveal his Son in me so that I might preach him among the Gentiles, my immediate response was not to consult any human being. I did not go up to Jerusalem to see those who were apostles before I was, but I went into Arabia. Later I returned to Damascus. Then after three years, I went up to Jerusalem to get acquainted with Cephas [that is, Peter] and stayed with him fifteen days. I saw none of the other apostles—only James, the Lord's brother. I assure you before God that what I am writing you is no lie. Then I went to Syria and Cilicia. I was personally unknown to the churches of Judea that are in Christ. They only heard the report: "The man who formerly persecuted us is now preaching the faith he once tried to destroy." And they praised God because of me. (Galatians 1:11-24)*

Because of his unique calling to be the Apostle to the Gentiles, Paul was to learn not simply from other Christians about the content of the gospel, but to spend a prolonged time learning directly from his new Lord. There was certainly nothing wrong in learning from other believers, but Paul needed to spend time sitting at Jesus' feet – much in the same way as the other disciples did during Jesus' earthly ministry. So, Paul chose not to head southwest to Jerusalem when he fled Damascus for his life, but rather southeast into the desert of Arabia. Paul's three years alone with Jesus – away from Jerusalem and the other disciples – mirrored the path of the those who lived intimately with Jesus in Galilee.

What did Paul learn from Jesus while in Arabia? Quite a lot! He had to learn what it meant to be Christ's chosen messenger to the Gentiles. He had to come to grips with the new covenant in Christ – that God had chosen to create one new humanity. The old distinctions and divisions between Jew and Gentile were broken down through the work of Jesus Christ. He had to study the Hebrew Scriptures to see how God's plan was foretold and how to communicate this in the most effective way. He had to come to grasp the incredible impact of the resurrection of Christ from the dead. And perhaps, most of all, Paul got to know Jesus Christ and he learned his life was no longer his own. As he said in his letters:

"For to me, to live is Christ and to die is gain." (Philippians 1:21)

"I have been crucified with Christ and I no longer live, but Christ lives in me. The life I now live in the body, I live by faith in the Son of God, who loved me and gave himself for me." (Galatians 2:20)

"But whatever were gains to me I now consider loss for the sake of Christ. What is more, I consider everything a loss because of the surpassing worth of knowing Christ Jesus my Lord, for whose sake I have lost all things. I consider them garbage, that I may gain Christ and be found in him, not having a righteousness of my own that comes from the law, but that which is through faith in Christ— the righteousness that comes from God on the basis of faith. I want to know Christ—yes, to know the power of his resurrection and participation in his sufferings, becoming like him in his death, and so, somehow, attaining to the resurrection from the dead. (Philippians 3:7-11)

It is impossible to know all that Paul learned in his "Arabian School" with Christ, but the rich gospel message given to him became clearly defined. The Lord inspired him to write everything we have from him in our New Testament. The doctrines of the absolute sovereignty of Christ, the unity of His Church, and salvation by faith and not through the observance of the law are all clearly seen in Paul's lifelong message. And his conduct in ministry – preaching to the Jew first and then the Gentile, not being a financial burden to those he preached to, and building teams of Christ followers as co-workers – possibly crystalized in his mind during these important three years in Arabia.

Barnabas

When it came time for Paul to come to Jerusalem as a believer in Christ, news of his conversion was met with skepticism. After all, he had been a persecutor and murderer of Christian believers. Many in the Jerusalem church would have had friends and relatives who had been imprisoned – perhaps even killed – by Saul of Tarsus. One of his early victims was the beloved deacon Stephen, one of the very first Christian martyrs. The book of Acts records Paul's first encounter with the Christians in Jerusalem.

> *When he came to Jerusalem, he tried to join the disciples, but they were all afraid of him, not believing that he really was a disciple. But Barnabas took him and brought him to the apostles. He told them how Saul on his journey had seen the Lord and that the Lord had spoken to him, and how in Damascus he had preached fearlessly in the name of Jesus. So Saul stayed with them and moved about freely in Jerusalem, speaking boldly in the name of the Lord. He talked and debated with the Hellenistic Jews, but they tried to kill him. When the believers learned of this, they took him down to Caesarea and sent him off to Tarsus.*
>
> *Then the church throughout Judea, Galilee and Samaria enjoyed a time of peace and was strengthened. Living in the fear of the Lord and encouraged by the Holy Spirit, it increased in numbers. (Acts 9:26-31)*

Barnabas was another unsung hero in Paul's life. This man played a key role in reconciliation and furtherance of Paul's ministry. Without the acceptance and endorsement of the Apostles in Jerusalem, Paul's ministry would have been severely impaired. Barnabas was loved and trusted by the entire church in Jerusalem. He was an encourager and a generous, selfless giver. The love of Barnabas made the difference. Barnabas had heard of Paul's Damascus road story and rejoiced in what God had done. Barnabas had also heard of how Paul had witnessed to the people in Damascus after his conversion.

So, Paul was accepted into the fellowship of the Jerusalem church and met with Peter, James the brother of Jesus, and perhaps some of the other Jerusalem believers. Soon thereafter, Paul brought forth evidence of his changed life by arguing with the Hellenistic Jews in Jerusalem, proclaiming boldly that Jesus was the Messiah throughout the city.

What followed in the wake of Paul's ministry became a pretty standard pattern. Violent opposition and strife followed Paul wherever he went. The Jews plotted to kill Paul, as they had in Damascus years earlier. Paul was now Public Enemy Number One to a completely different group of people. To protect Paul (and perhaps also to restore some peace in Jerusalem), the disciples sent Paul off to his home town of Tarsus.

I always chuckle when I read of the result of Paul leaving Jerusalem. *"Then the church throughout Judea, Galilee and Samaria enjoyed a time of peace... ."* (Acts 9:31) Paul left

Switchbacks

Jerusalem and the church enjoyed a time of peace. There had to be a connection between these two events. Perhaps everyone breathed a sigh of relief! Paul was a fearless agitator, and the Lord used this throughout his life to spread the gospel.

Sometime later, as the Christian message spread beyond Jerusalem, there developed a strong Christian fellowship to the north in the city of Antioch, a city not far from Tarsus. Some of the Christians not only preached the gospel to Jews, but also to Greek Gentiles. And many of them accepted the message and became followers of Christ. This new and astounding development caused the Apostles in Jerusalem to send Barnabas to investigate. Barnabas saw the Lord's hand was at work and encouraged the church there.

Barnabas realized there was an opportunity to strengthen and grow the young Antioch church, so he went to Tarsus and found Paul. He brought him to Antioch and the two worked together. For the following year, Barnabas and Paul taught the people. Believers were first called Christians in Antioch. (Acts 11:26) When a famine threatened the region around Jerusalem, the Antioch church raised money and sent it to believers there in the hands of Barnabas and Paul. (Acts 11:30)

Paul's ministry to the Gentiles had begun. For the rest of his life he would be on the move for the Lord.

Life as a Missionary

Early in his Christian walk, Paul was told by the Lord he would be a messenger to the Gentiles, and at Antioch this work had begun. The Gentile world was a large one – much larger than the Jewish world that Paul knew well. It had to be an overwhelming task that may have weighed heavily upon him. How would this ministry unfold? Where would he start and where would he go? What was to be his strategy?

While ministering in Antioch to the church there, Paul began to get answers.

> *Now in the church at Antioch there were prophets and teachers: Barnabas, Simeon called Niger, Lucius of Cyrene, Manaen (who had been brought up with Herod the tetrarch) and Saul. While they were worshiping the Lord and fasting, the Holy Spirit said, "Set apart for me Barnabas and Saul for the work to which I have called them." So after they had fasted and prayed, they placed their hands on them and sent them off. (Acts 13:1-3)*

Barnabas and Paul were sent off from Antioch to spread the gospel to new places. What a unique adventure! They were an ancient spiritual version of the Lewis and Clark expedition. They were to be trailblazers for Christ, and they were led by the Holy Spirit to sail to Cyprus, Barnabas' home island. Barnabas and Paul had the young John Mark as their companion. Their starting point in proclaiming the gospel of Jesus Christ was to speak in the Jewish synagogues everywhere they went. (Acts 13:5) Barnabas and Paul eventually came to the important city of Paphos, and an opportunity for God to work dramatically through Paul presented itself.

> *They traveled through the whole island until they came to Paphos. There they met a Jewish sorcerer and false prophet named Bar-Jesus, who was an attendant of the proconsul, Sergius Paulus. The proconsul, an intelligent man, sent for Barnabas and Saul because he wanted to hear the word of God. But Elymas the sorcerer (for that is what his name means) opposed them and tried to turn the proconsul from the faith. Then Saul, who was also called Paul, filled with the Holy Spirit, looked straight at Elymas and said, "You are a child of the devil and an enemy of everything that is right! You are full of all kinds of deceit and trickery. Will you never stop perverting the right ways of the Lord? Now the hand of the Lord is against you. You are going to be blind for a time, not even able to see the light of the sun."*
>
> *Immediately mist and darkness came over him, and he groped about, seeking someone to lead him by the hand. When the proconsul saw what had happened, he believed, for he was amazed at the teaching about the Lord. (Acts 13:6-12)*

It was apparent that Paul took the lead in this situation, which is not surprising, given what we know of his personality. God was working mightily through Paul's speaking and actions. From this point on, Paul's name is mentioned first. "Barnabas and Paul" became "Paul and his companions." (Acts 13:13) Paul was the speaker and Barnabas used his gifts of encouragement and teaching to help establish the churches.

Paul and Barnabas left Cyprus and sailed to the mainland, preaching the gospel in the region known as Galatia. Their young companion, John Mark, left them shortly after they left Cyprus. It appeared the stress of ministry was too much for the young man, at least at this point in his life. In what was later to be known as Paul's first missionary journey, they preached the gospel in many towns, performed many miracles to substantiate their message, established small churches comprised of both Jews and Gentiles, while facing times of opposition and life-threatening persecution. At one point along the way in the town of Lystra, Paul was stoned and left for dead by his attackers.

Switchbacks

Early on, Paul was shown how much he would have to suffer for the name of Christ, as was foretold shortly after his radical spiritual "about face." (Acts 9:16)

What was the content of the gospel message Paul preached? We are fortunate to have a few sermons preached by Paul in the book of Acts. We can read two of these sermons in Acts 13:16-41, and in Acts 26:1-29.

Central points of Paul's gospel message included:

- The Old Testament Scriptures point to the coming of a Messiah who will save Israel and all the nations from their sins. Jesus is that Messiah, the Son of God. God has made this certain by many signs and testimonies, and most importantly, raising Jesus from the dead.

- Believing in Jesus brings forgiveness of sins because of his shed blood on our behalf.

- Believing in Jesus also brings the entrance of the Holy Spirit in each believer, which was promised by God in the Scriptures. This enables believers to live lives pleasing to God.

- Believing in Jesus ensures that we too will be raised from the dead and have everlasting life.

- This salvation comes through faith alone in Jesus Christ and not through mere observance of the Jewish law.

While a large part of Paul's ministry was planting churches, he still felt the need to support and shepherd them after they had been established. Before the end of his first missionary journey, Paul returned to the Galatian towns *"strengthening the disciples and encouraging them to remain true to the faith."* (Acts 14:22) Paul and Barnabas appointed elders in each church. When Paul and Barnabas eventually returned to Antioch, they shared with the entire church that God *"had opened the door of faith to the Gentiles."* (Acts 14:27)

The Gentile question – the Council at Jerusalem

Having Gentiles come to faith in Christ was not something all Jewish Christians accepted readily. It would have been wonderful if everyone came to believe Paul's gospel message was the only true message, but no "straight-path" acceptance occurred. The premise was open for debate that salvation was through faith in Christ alone, and not through faith plus observance of the Jewish law. The truth was clear to Paul, but not to others apart from his ministry. Even in the early Christian church, opposition and pondering ensued.

In Acts 15, we read about an important council convened in Jerusalem to address the Gentile question. After much debate, Peter and the other Apostles decided that God did not require Gentiles to observe every aspect of the Jewish law in order to be truly saved. Salvation and justification was by faith alone, but Gentile believers had to recognize the law was *"holy, righteous and good."* (Romans 7:12) Although this pronouncement settled the issue officially, the "Jesus plus the law" doctrine was something Paul would fight against his entire life. His opponents became known as *"those of the circumcision group."* (Titus 1:10) There would always be Christians who sought to impose extra rules upon those with different backgrounds. Sadly, we have people who still try to do this today.

Paul's life would have been so much simpler and more peace-filled if some Jewish believers had not insisted upon holding on to the Mosaic law and seeking to impose it upon all Christians. He had to fight this fight constantly through his preaching and through his letters. At one point, he even had to confront Peter who was living in a hypocritical manner.

> *When Cephas [that is, Peter] came to Antioch, I opposed him to his face, because he stood condemned. For before certain men came from James, he used to eat with the Gentiles. But when they arrived, he began to draw back and separate himself from the Gentiles because he was afraid of those who belonged to the circumcision group. The other Jews joined him in his hypocrisy, so that by their hypocrisy even Barnabas was led astray.*
>
> *When I saw that they were not acting in line with the truth of the gospel, I said to Cephas in front of them all, "You are a Jew, yet you live like a Gentile and not like a Jew. How is it, then, that you force Gentiles to follow Jewish customs?*
>
> *We who are Jews by birth and not sinful Gentiles know that a person is not justified by the works of the law, but by faith in Jesus Christ. So we, too, have put our faith in Christ Jesus that we may be justified by faith in Christ and not by the works of the law, because by the works of the law no one will be justified."*
> *(Galatians 2:11-15)*

I am impressed with Paul's courage to confront Peter publicly and his unwavering commitment to his convictions based upon truth. He certainly was a man capable of righteous indignation! Salvation is through Jesus Christ alone and not through our works or observance of the law. Christians were to preach this through their words and their actions.

Paul's Travels and Travails

Paul was later to embark on several other missionary journeys, and the latter pages of the book of Acts – indeed, great portions of the New Testament – are dominated with the events of his life and ministry.

Paul's life as a missionary did not contain many straight paths. His road was winding and hard, yet full of power and grace. Before the start of his second journey, he had a sharp disagreement with Barnabas over the young John Mark, who had deserted them during their first missionary journey. Barnabas wanted to bring the young man, but Paul refused. Perhaps Barnabas focused upon the needs of the young disciple, while Paul focused upon the needs of the work at hand. The two co-workers had a strong disagreement over Mark and parted company. We have no record that the two ever worked together again.

Yet Paul greatly valued team ministry. Wherever he traveled, he tried to have faithful companions to labor alongside him. Silas, Timothy, Luke and many others were an important part of his ministry. At the end of his life, Paul even desired Mark to be with him. (II Timothy 4:11) Paul was a team player and team builder – a multiplier, not a "monopolizer" of ministry.

He did not always know where the Lord was leading him and his small band of helpers. During his second missionary journey, there was a time where the Holy Spirit prevented Paul from moving into certain regions, but instead led him in new, far-reaching directions.

> *Paul and his companions traveled throughout the region of Phrygia and Galatia, having been kept by the Holy Spirit from preaching the word in the province of Asia. When they came to the border of Mysia, they tried to enter Bithynia, but the Spirit of Jesus would not allow them to. So they passed by Mysia and went down to Troas. During the night Paul had a vision of a man of Macedonia standing and begging him, "Come over to Macedonia and help us."*

After Paul had seen the vision, we got ready at once to leave for Macedonia, concluding that God had called us to preach the gospel to them. (Acts 16:6-10)

Paul's life was one spirit-led adventure after another, never really seeing where the road ahead would lead. And many times, it led him into perilous situations. The catalogue of his suffering is long and harrowing to contemplate.

Five times I received from the Jews the forty lashes minus one. Three times I was beaten with rods, once I was pelted with stones, three times I was shipwrecked, I spent a night and a day in the open sea, I have been constantly on the move. I have been in danger from rivers, in danger from bandits, in danger from my fellow Jews, in danger from Gentiles; in danger in the city, in danger in the country, in danger at sea; and in danger from false believers. I have labored and toiled and have often gone without sleep; I have known hunger and thirst and have often gone without food; I have been cold and naked. Besides everything else, I face daily the pressure of my concern for all the churches. Who is weak, and I do not feel weak? Who is led into sin, and I do not inwardly burn?

If I must boast, I will boast of the things that show my weakness. The God and Father of the Lord Jesus, who is to be praised forever, knows that I am not lying. In Damascus the governor under King Aretas had the city of the Damascenes guarded in order to arrest me. But I was lowered in a basket from a window in the wall and slipped through his hands. (II Corinthians 11:24-33)

We may know of Paul's many physical sufferings and harrowing experiences, but in the passage above he also mentioned the mental burden he carried for his pastoral concern for all the churches he had helped establish. As he said, it was a "daily pressure." He carried a heavy load. Modern-day pastors know of this concern as well!

Paul's mission was to preach the gospel to the Gentiles, and with that came trekking over large portions of the Roman Empire, establishing churches, defending sound doctrine with new believers, spending large amounts of time in prison, and facing death at the hands of his countrymen and the Romans. Some of his life experiences seemed to impede his God-given task. How could the gospel spread, for example, while he was locked in a prison cell? Yet, Paul's attitude did not reflect frustration or anger. He writes to the church in Philippi about being in chains.

Now I want you to know, brothers and sisters, that what has happened to me has actually served to advance the gospel. As a result, it has become clear throughout the whole palace guard and to everyone else that I am in chains for Christ. And because of my chains, most of the brothers and sisters have become confident in the Lord and dare all the more to proclaim the gospel without fear.

It is true that some preach Christ out of envy and rivalry, but others out of goodwill. The latter do so out of love, knowing that I am put here for the defense of the gospel. The former preach Christ out of selfish ambition, not sincerely, supposing that they can stir up trouble for me while I am in chains. But what does it matter? The important thing is that in every way, whether from false motives or true, Christ is preached. And because of this I rejoice. (Philippians 1:12-15)

Like Joseph in Egypt many generations earlier, Paul was willing to accept that even living in a prison cell could be God's will for him. Others meant it for evil, but God meant it for good.

And there are hints Paul also suffered some sort of physical infirmity – a "thorn in the flesh," as he described it. In his second letter to the church in Corinth, Paul speaks of special revelations he received from the Lord and how God kept him humble.

I must go on boasting. Although there is nothing to be gained, I will go on to visions and revelations from the Lord. I know a man in Christ who fourteen years ago was caught up to the third heaven. Whether it was in the body or out of the body I do not know—God knows. And I know that this man—whether in the body or apart from the body I do not know, but God knows – was caught up to paradise and heard inexpressible things, things that no one is permitted to tell. I will boast about a man like that, but I will not boast about myself, except about my weaknesses. Even if I should choose to boast, I would not be a fool, because I would be speaking the truth. But I refrain, so no one will think more of me than is warranted by what I do or say, or because of these surpassingly great revelations. Therefore, in order to keep me from becoming conceited, I was given a thorn in my flesh, a messenger of Satan, to torment me. Three times I pleaded with the Lord to take it away from me. But he said to me, "My grace is sufficient for you, for my power is made perfect in weakness." Therefore I will boast all the more gladly about my weaknesses, so that Christ's power may rest on me. That is why, for Christ's sake, I delight in weaknesses, in insults, in hardships, in persecutions, in difficulties. For when I am weak, then I am strong. (II Corinthians 12:1-10)

The great paradox in Paul's life was strength through weakness. A man who had every reason to "throw his spiritual weight around" because of his gifts, experiences, background and accomplishments refused to do so. Therein lies the greatness of the Apostle Paul.

The End of the Line

The Bible does not tell us how or when Paul died. Wouldn't we like to know! But once again, we are reminded that the story of the Bible is not about Paul or any individual, but about the purposes of God. Church tradition tells us he died a martyr's death in Rome after a long imprisonment.

In his last letter to his spiritual son Timothy, Paul wrote of the end of his life. He gave Timothy advice about how to conduct his own ministry going forward – advice Timothy would have recognized as advice Paul himself lived by.

In the presence of God and of Christ Jesus, who will judge the living and the dead, and in view of his appearing and his kingdom, I give you this charge: Preach the word; be prepared in season and out of season; correct, rebuke and encourage—with great patience and careful instruction. For the time will come when people will not put up with sound doctrine. Instead, to suit their own desires, they will gather around them a great number of teachers to say what their itching ears want to hear. They will turn their ears away from the truth and turn aside to myths. But you, keep your head in all situations, endure hardship, do the work of an evangelist, discharge all the duties of your ministry.

For I am already being poured out like a drink offering, and the time for my departure is near. I have fought the good fight, I have finished the race, I have kept the faith. Now there is in store for me the crown of righteousness, which the Lord, the righteous Judge, will award to me on that day—and not only to me, but also to all who have longed for his appearing. (II Timothy 4:1-8)

What is most remarkable is that Paul reached the end of his life with his principles and values intact. As he said to one king during a trial toward the end of his life *"I was not disobedient to the vision from heaven."* (Acts 26:19)

Next to the Lord Jesus himself, perhaps there is no one in the New Testament that can be more admired. Here are some takeaways from this remarkable life:

Switchbacks

- God's choice of Saul of Tarsus to preach the gospel to the Gentiles on the surface made no sense at all. But in hindsight, it was an ingenious choice. God not only used Paul's mind, but his tempestuous personality to build His kingdom. He transformed this driven, bigoted Pharisee into an effective instrument to spread the Gospel of Christ throughout the Roman Empire. What a surprising and unlikely choice! We should not be too surprised when God calls a person to do something that seems illogical to the human mind. God has gifted each of us with our own peculiar gifts and abilities, and He calls us and enables us to use them for his glory – sometimes in surprising ways!

- Paul's life was marked by the faithful actions of "unsung heroes." We should remember the brave forgiveness of Ananias, the unnamed strong-armed men who let him down from the walls of Damascus in a basket, and the encouraging, loving acceptance of Barnabas. Perhaps God would call us to be such an unsung hero in the life of another.

- Paul learned from the outset of his ministry that God would best accomplish His work through a team rather than through the efforts of just a single person. Paul's list of co-workers was a long one. When we seek to minister in the Lord's name, we should realize we need our fellow brothers and sisters to do the work effectively. When working in ministry teams, we build one another up, bolster one another's weaknesses, and encourage one another along the way. Paul not only taught this truth in his letters, like in I Corinthians 12, but lived it out in front of everyone day in and day out. We need to repent of our rugged Christian individualism and see the biblical pattern for ministry modeled by the Apostle Paul.

- Paul's life after the Damascus road experience was one marked by the grace of God. *"But by the grace of God, I am what I am."* (I Corinthians 15:10) Paul never forgot what Christ had saved him from, and he never was set off course from his mission. Remembering our own spiritual history and how the grace of God has transformed us can rekindle our love and the gifts God has given us, renewing our zeal and desire to serve Him.

- Like Jesus, Paul learned obedience through what he suffered. Paul discovered that the victorious life in Christ was not an easy life, nor is it a straight road. Was there ever a tougher man than Paul? He moved from a life where he was in total control to a life where Jesus was in total control. His transformed life entailed suffering, but great eternal reward. Let us go and do likewise!

Questions for Reflection and Discussion

1. God used Paul's upbringing and unique personality to accomplish His purposes. Reflect upon your own background and personality. How might God be able to use you in unique ways?

2. Many people were shocked at the drastic change in Paul's life after his Damascus Road experience. Have you ever witnessed a God-initiated change in a person that surprised you? Have you ever been surprised at who God chooses to accomplish certain tasks? If so, what was your response?

3. There were unsung heroes in Paul's life – most notably, Barnabas. Reflect upon Barnabas' role in Paul's life. Are there ways you can be an encouraging person to others? Have you had a "Barnabas" in your life?

4. Paul embraced team ministry as a model for doing God's work and spreading the gospel. He was a multiplier, not a "monopolizer" of ministry. How easy is it for you to work in a team situation? Is your preference to work in a team or alone?

5. Paul was able to communicate the central truths of the gospel consistently. Take some time to develop in your own words a synopsis of the Christian gospel.

6. Paul suffered many trials throughout his lifetime. What sustained him? What lessons can we draw from his experience?

Switchbacks

12

The Purposeful Journey: JESUS

"He has done everything well." (Mark 7:37)

The Lord Jesus lived a perfect life. No sin or bad decisions. The people who witnessed Jesus in action exclaimed, *"He has done everything well."* (Mark 7:37) Yet by the Father's design, Jesus' life was also full of crooked paths. One would think the Son of God would not have unexpected twists and turns throughout His life, but He did. We read in the book of Hebrews that Jesus *"learned obedience from what he suffered."* (Hebrews 5:8) And suffering sometimes meant a winding path.

The Young Life of a Refugee

In our prior discussion of the life of Mary, we saw that Jesus was born into a refugee family. He went to Egypt shortly after his birth in Bethlehem, and eventually settled in Nazareth. Poverty, uncertainty, danger, and complete reliance upon God's protection were all part of Jesus' life from the beginning. When Jesus started his ministry, he did not own property or have much in worldly possessions. As He said to one of his would-be disciples:

> *"Foxes have dens and birds have nests, but the Son of Man has no place to lay his head." (Matthew 8:20)*

We love to be in control in life – we want to have a nice home, security, and plans for the future. Jesus did not seem to value these things the way we do. He had no place to lay His head. Even most animals have this much security.

On the surface, it appeared that Jesus lived a subsistence lifestyle. By earthly standards he was a pauper. He was the son of a carpenter who did not pursue this as a career. Such a lifestyle did not lend itself to predictability and security.

Yet, He was the Son of God. Paul wrote that although Jesus was equal to God, He made Himself nothing, emptying Himself for our sake.

Who, being in very nature God, did not consider equality with God something to be used to his own advantage; rather, he made himself nothing by taking the very nature of a servant, being made in human likeness. And being found in appearance as a man, he humbled himself by becoming obedient to death – even death on a cross! Therefore God exalted him to the highest place and gave him the name that is above every name, that at the name of Jesus every knee should bow, in heaven and on earth and under the earth, and every tongue acknowledge that Jesus Christ is Lord, to the glory of God the Father. (Philippians 2:6-11)

Starting in the Wilderness

After Jesus' baptism by John the Baptist, He was led into the wilderness to be tempted by the Devil. After fasting forty days, Jesus met Satan, and three times the Devil tempted Him to take some shortcuts – to create His own straight pathways. You can read the account in Matthew 4:1-11, Mark 1:12-13, and Luke 4:1-13.

The first temptation hit Jesus at the gut level, quite literally. Satan spoke to Him:

"Are you hungry, Jesus? Since you are the Son of God, feed yourself. Turn these stones to bread."

Jesus could have easily fed Himself in this situation. After all, later in His ministry He miraculously fed thousands of hungry people to meet physical needs. Yet He discerned His Father wanted Him to wait upon His provision and not act selfishly on His own behalf. Jesus harkened back to Israel's time in the wilderness, when God provided for His people in His own unique way – with manna from heaven. Moses' words spoken to the people of Israel came to the Lord's mind clearly at this time:

He humbled you, causing you to hunger and then feeding you with manna, which neither you nor your ancestors had known, to teach you that man does not live on bread alone but on every word that comes from the mouth of the LORD. Your clothes did not wear out and your feet did not swell during these forty years. Know then in your heart that as a man disciplines his son, so the LORD your God disciplines you. (Deuteronomy 8:3-5)

Jesus realized the physical hunger He was experiencing was to teach Him to rely upon His Father's provision – to wait on God's timing and plan. So, He declined Satan's first offer.

Satan came back with another "straight path" suggestion. He miraculously took Jesus from the desert to the highest peak of the temple in Jerusalem, and challenged Him

Switchbacks

to perform a public miracle so stupendous that the Jews would have to believe He was the Messiah. Satan said something like this:

> *"Throw yourself off this parapet and show yourself to all the people that you are the Son of God. After all, it says in Scripture that God will send his angels to protect you – you won't so much as stub your toe! Then God's plan will be established – everyone will acknowledge that you are the Son of God when you make such a dramatic media splash."*

Satan was proposing another attractive shortcut. Jesus knew God's real plan was for Him to suffer and die on a cross so the sins of the world could be atoned for, and that through this people would come to have faith in Him. God's path was one of pain and suffering; the Devil's alternative must have been extremely appealing. Why not do something publicly to show how God would deliver His Son? That would impress people!

But Jesus did not take the bait. He once again recalled the words of Moses, when He told Satan He would not test the Lord in such a way.

> *Do not follow other gods, the gods of the peoples around you; for the LORD your God, who is among you, is a jealous God and his anger will burn against you, and he will destroy you from the face of the land. Do not put the LORD your God to the test as you did at Massah. Be sure to keep the commands of the LORD your God and the stipulations and decrees he has given you. Do what is right and good in the LORD's sight, so that it may go well with you and you may go in and take over the good land the LORD promised on oath to your ancestors, thrusting out all your enemies before you, as the LORD said. (Deuteronomy 6:14-19)*

At Massah, the people of Israel were ready to kill Moses because they had no water. They failed to believe God would provide for them, and they tested the Lord's patience by their lack of faith. This is what Jesus recalled when answering Satan a second time. He was not going to test his Father by taking such a shortcut. He trusted that God would work out His plan in His good time.

Satan and Jesus would go one more round in the wilderness. Perhaps the Devil thought the third time would be the charm. Satan once again miraculously transported Jesus to a place where He was able to see all the kingdoms and splendor of the world. He was good at special effects. He tempted Jesus a third time with words something like these:

> *"I know, Jesus, that your goal is to be King of Kings and Lord of Lords. It is God's plan that you rule over all the earth. Look at all this! I can give this to you. All you need to do is bow down and worship me. How does that sound?"*

Satan was telling Jesus the ends justify the means. This was the ultimate temptation for Jesus to take a shortcut to His life's destiny. Satan was later called by Jesus *"the prince of this world,"* (John 12:31 and John 14:30) but the Devil was not the King and Absolute Sovereign. Satan was lying, and Jesus saw through it right away. If He were to bow down and worship the Devil, Jesus would not ultimately rule over all – Satan would. Jesus quickly saw through the deception and quoted Moses' teaching a third time:

> *Fear the LORD your God, serve him only and take your oaths in his name. (Deuteronomy 6:13)*

Jesus commanded Satan to get lost, and the Devil had to obey. This fight was over – for the time being. Jesus had refused to walk the easy, straight trail the Devil had presented to Him. He chose His Father's winding path instead.

The Purposeful Yet Unhurried Life

You may be familiar with Rick Warren's book *The Purpose Driven Life*. Jesus' life was purposeful, true, but perhaps not driven the way we Americans use that word! His life was purposeful, yet patient and unhurried. As we read through the gospel accounts, we see that Jesus never seemed to be anxious about His itinerary. If wristwatches or appointment calendars were around in those days, Jesus would not have owned them. Unlike a lot of modern-day pilgrims, He *walked* through the Holy Land; He didn't *run*. One of my former pastors went to the Holy Land, and when he came back, he describes his trip like this: *"I ran today where Jesus walked."* There was a patient quality about Jesus' ministry, but always with a higher purpose. We never see Him perturbed by interruptions or vexed with His schedule.

Instead, we see in Scripture that Jesus was never in a hurry, nor quick to take advantage of capitalizing on publicity. If Jesus had hired a publicity agent at the outset of his ministry, this person no doubt would have been exasperated. At every step Jesus seemed to make political errors to damage His image. Here are just a few short examples.

Switchbacks

When having success and notoriety in Peter's hometown of Capernaum, the people there tried to persuade Him to stay and perform more miracles. Jesus refused.

At daybreak, Jesus went out to a solitary place. The people were looking for him and when they came to where he was, they tried to keep him from leaving them. But he said, "I must proclaim the good news of the kingdom of God to the other towns also, because that is why I was sent." And he kept on preaching in the synagogues of Judea. (Luke 4:42-44)

After feeding the five thousand, the crowds wanted to make Him king. Jesus would have none of it.

After the people saw the sign Jesus performed, they began to say, "Surely this is the Prophet who is to come into the world." Jesus, knowing that they intended to come and make him king by force, withdrew again to a mountain by himself. (John 6:14-15)

When evil spirits cried out identifying Him as the Son of God, He commanded them to keep quiet about it.

Whenever the impure spirits saw him, they fell down before him and cried out, "You are the Son of God." But he gave them strict orders not to tell others about him. (Mark 3:11-12)

When His own disciples proclaimed He was the Son of God, He told them to keep it to themselves for a time.

"But what about you?" he asked. "Who do you say I am?"

Simon Peter answered, "You are the Messiah, the Son of the living God."

Jesus replied, "Blessed are you, Simon son of Jonah, for this was not revealed to you by flesh and blood, but by my Father in heaven. And I tell you that you are Peter, and on this rock I will build my church, and the gates of Hades will not overcome it. I will give you the keys of the kingdom of heaven; whatever you bind on earth will be bound in heaven, and whatever you loose on earth will be loosed in heaven." Then he ordered his disciples not to tell anyone that he was the Messiah. (Matthew 16:15-20)

And Jesus seemed never to view an encounter with anyone to be a bother to His schedule. When interrupted by children in the midst of His ministry in the Jerusalem temple, the disciples became irate at the intrusion. Jesus remained unperturbed.

> *People were also bringing babies to Jesus for him to place his hands on them. When the disciples saw this, they rebuked them. But Jesus called the children to him and said, "Let the little children come to me, and do not hinder them, for the kingdom of God belongs to such as these. Truly I tell you, anyone who will not receive the kingdom of God like a little child will never enter it." (Luke 18:15-17)*

When an uninvited prostitute interrupted a dinner party at the home of a man, and she began to anoint His feet, Jesus affirmed her actions and did not allow them to interfere with her act of worship.

> *"Leave her alone," said Jesus. "Why are you bothering her? She has done a beautiful thing to me. The poor you will always have with you, and you can help them any time you want. But you will not always have me. She did what she could. She poured perfume on my body beforehand to prepare for my burial. Truly I tell you, wherever the gospel is preached throughout the world, what she has done will also be told, in memory of her." (Mark 14:6-9)*

Examining Jesus' ministry, we see He valued individual people first, and His schedule was a distant second.

Two stories especially illustrate Jesus' patient refusal to walk straight paths in His life because of His higher purpose. The first is the story of the dead girl and the sick woman. It is told in three of the four gospel accounts. (Matthew 9:20–22; Mark 5:25–34; and Luke 8:43–48)

At one point in Jesus' ministry, He was surrounded by a large crowd at the side of the Sea of Galilee. In the middle of this hustle and bustle, a synagogue ruler names Jairus came to Jesus and fell at His feet. Jairus begged Jesus to come to his home and heal his daughter who was near death. Time was of the essence, so Jairus thought. The precious little girl needed a touch from Jesus' hand. It was her only hope.

Jesus agreed to go with Jairus. It was a perfectly appropriate time to hurry! The child was very sick and needed to be healed. Yet the large crowd must have slowed down the progress – perhaps much to the fear and frustration of Jairus and the disciples.

Meanwhile, in the middle of the large crowd there was another suffering person – a woman who had been bleeding for twelve years. Isn't it interesting that the little girl was twelve and this woman had suffered for twelve years? This poor woman had suffered for the entire time Jairus' daughter had been alive! She had been through many unsuccessful treatments at the hands of doctors who could do nothing for her. After seeing these physicians and probably paying high medical fees, she only had grown worse. Because of her bleeding, she was ceremonially unclean and treated as an outcast and second-class citizen in the Jewish community. She was desperate and came to the conclusion that she only needed to touch Jesus' cloak and she would be healed. There was no need to interrupt Jesus who was running an urgent errand.

And this is what she did. She touched Jesus' garment and immediately she was healed. It would have sufficed if her story ended there. A nice, straight-path story if ever there was one. But Jesus had other plans.

> *At once Jesus realized that power had gone out from him. He turned around in the crowd and asked, "Who touched my clothes?"*
>
> *"You see the people crowding against you," his disciples answered, "and yet you can ask, 'Who touched me?'"*
>
> *But Jesus kept looking around to see who had done it. Then the woman, knowing what had happened to her, came and fell at his feet and, trembling with fear, told him the whole truth. He said to her, "Daughter, your faith has healed you. Go in peace and be freed from your suffering." (Mark 5:30-34)*

Jesus stopped the procession to Jairus' house and demanded an audience with the woman. Many were undoubtedly thinking: "What about the little girl and the urgent need awaiting Jesus at Jairus' home?" But the woman was not going to be allowed to go unnoticed. She had to go public. Jesus had stopped the show until He unveiled who He had just healed. Of course, He knew, but He wanted to say more to the healed woman.

And what a beautiful encounter it was! The woman, perhaps mortified by the attention amidst the crowd, came and fell at Jesus' feet and told her entire story to the Lord. All her pain over the last twelve years spilled out at the feet of the Great Physician. Jesus showed love and compassion for this poor woman and sent her away in peace.

But this delay had cost precious time. And during these few minutes, word arrived that Jairus' daughter had died. The messengers who brought the news told Jairus there was no need to trouble Jesus any longer. It was too late.

But again, Jesus had other plans.

> *Overhearing what they said, Jesus told him, "Don't be afraid; just believe."*

> He did not let anyone follow him except Peter, James and John the brother of James. When they came to the home of the synagogue leader, Jesus saw a commotion, with people crying and wailing loudly. He went in and said to them, "Why all this commotion and wailing? The child is not dead but asleep." But they laughed at him.
>
> After he put them all out, he took the child's father and mother and the disciples who were with him, and went in where the child was. He took her by the hand and said to her, "Talitha koum!" (which means "Little girl, I say to you, get up!"). Immediately the girl stood up and began to walk around (she was twelve years old). At this they were completely astonished. He gave strict orders not to let anyone know about this, and told them to give her something to eat. (Mark 5:36-43)

Jesus used the circumstances to perform even a greater miracle – the raising of this dead girl. His unhurried approach put people first and time-bound agendas further down on His priority list. The shortest distance between two points is a straight path. But when you are God, time and distance are of no concern.

Another story is perhaps an even clearer illustration of Jesus' lack of adherence to human schedules and agendas. The story of Lazarus, Mary and Martha is well-known and told in John Chapter 11.

Three of Jesus' best friends were members of one family. Siblings Mary, Martha and Lazarus lived in the tiny village of Bethany outside of Jerusalem. Jesus loved them all deeply; Mary was a woman who had anointed Jesus' feet with expensive perfume earlier in His ministry, and He had eaten in their home at least on one occasion. Jesus received word from the sisters that Lazarus was very ill and perilously close to death. They begged Jesus to come at once to heal Lazarus. They had faith that Jesus could do this and he was their last hope.

Jesus made a bold statement, showing that He knew what He was going to do. His subsequent actions did not involve a straight path, however.

> When he heard this, Jesus said, "This sickness will not end in death. No, it is for God's glory so that God's Son may be glorified through it." (John 11:4)

Upon receiving the news about Lazarus, Jesus' actions are puzzling. He stayed where He was for two more days before heading for the home of His friends. If Jesus was intending to heal Lazarus, everyone would expect Him to hurry to his bedside in

Bethany. Then after two days of doing nothing, Jesus announced He was going to journey to Bethany.

This presented a dilemma for Jesus and His disciples. Jesus' life had been threatened by many of the Jews in Judea, and to return to this region put Him in grave danger. To put it mildly, the disciples thought that going to Bethany was a very bad idea.

At this point in the story, Jesus is causing everyone great anxiety. Mary and Martha are wondering what is keeping the Lord, and His disciples are questioning His wisdom for walking into peril in the presence of His enemies. Thomas even made a fatalistic pronouncement: *"Let us also go, that we may die with him."* (John 11:16)

Jesus' way of doing things seems totally different from everyone else's around Him. His timetable was unique and unduplicated. Yet, Jesus' way was not without purpose.

When Jesus finally arrived at Bethany, Lazarus had been dead and buried for four days. Many mourners had gathered to comfort the two sisters. When each sister met Jesus, they both said the same thing to Him: *"Lord, if you had been here, my brother would not have died." (John 11:21, 32)* This was an expression of their hope and expectation for Jesus to have walked a simple, straight path in the midst of their family crisis. But Jesus lovingly failed to do this. He had greater things in mind.

We know the rest of the story. Jesus proclaimed Himself the resurrection and the life to Martha, and He backed it up by miraculously raising Lazarus from the dead. No one present expected Jesus to do this. Jesus knew this was His Father's plan all along. Sometimes the crooked trail brings God greater glory than the straight one.

The Time for a Straight Path

Jesus lived an unhurried life, yet when it was time to go to His death, there were no delays or detours. He told His disciples this repeatedly in the gospels.

> *As the time approached for him to be taken up to heaven, Jesus resolutely set out for Jerusalem. (Luke 9:51)*

> *"In any case, I must press on today and tomorrow and the next day—for surely no prophet can die outside Jerusalem!" (Luke 13:33)*

When Jesus knew it was time to die, no one could dissuade Him. His disciples tried, and He even wrestled with the ordeal in the Garden of Gethsemane. On the night of His betrayal and arrest, His disciples slept and then fled, while Jesus prayed and then endured.

"Father, if you are willing, take this cup from me; yet not my will, but yours be done." (Luke 22:42)

When one reads the account of Jesus' trial and crucifixion, one cannot help but wonder who was really on trial. Was it Jesus or the rest of humanity? Jesus is in complete control at every step of His Passion. But look at the zigs and zags in Jesus' trial. He is yanked around from Jews to Romans and back again. There were few straight pathways in His trial and execution. His prolonged torture and suffering had to be excruciating. Yet in every circumstance throughout His life, Jesus trusted His Father's provision, timetable, and plan. And at the end, the straight path to the cross had to be taken. His blood had to be shed. And then it was finished. Salvation was accomplished in the most incredible way.

The End of the Line

Any reading of the gospel accounts shows us clearly that Jesus' ways were not our ways. And yet, He did all things well.

Instead of a purpose-*driven* life, Jesus led a purposeful, patient and obedient life, trusting in the timing of His Father. The "unhurried" quality of Jesus' ministry is apparent – not without purpose, just resting in His Father's timing. Jesus trusted God's process. He embraced the divine winding trail completely.

There are many examples in the gospels of Jesus avoiding "straight path" thinking. He was tempted to take shortcuts by Satan in the wilderness – to let the end justify the means, but He did not succumb. He did not yield to the desires of the crowds or even His disciples to become a military ruler. And He certainly did not bow to the traditions of the Pharisees and live according to their rigid traditions. His only concern was to do the will of His Father. Jesus chose His Father's way, and He did not seek straight paths.

Perhaps the most surprising "switchback" of all time came on that first Easter Sunday morning, when Jesus rose from the dead. It certainly took Satan by surprise! God snatched victory out of the jaws of defeat. This turn of events is unequaled in history. Paul wrote about the significance of this truth to our Christian faith in a letter to the church in Corinth.

> *And if Christ has not been raised, our preaching is useless and so is your faith. More than that, we are then found to be false witnesses about God, for we have testified about God that he raised Christ from the dead. But he did not raise him if in fact the dead are not raised. For if the dead are not raised, then Christ has*

not been raised either. And if Christ has not been raised, your faith is futile; you are still in your sins. Then those also who have fallen asleep in Christ are lost. If only for this life we have hope in Christ, we are of all people most to be pitied.

But Christ has indeed been raised from the dead, the firstfruits of those who have fallen asleep. For since death came through a man, the resurrection of the dead comes also through a man. For as in Adam all die, so in Christ all will be made alive. (1 Corinthians 15:14-22)

The greatest comfort we can receive in life is to know we have been made alive in Christ. And because of the Resurrection, all our crooked paths will one day make sense when we are made fully alive for all eternity.

Questions for Reflection and Discussion

1. Jesus' humble beginnings and "subsistence lifestyle" are clearly outlined in the Bible. Why do you suppose God chose for Jesus to live this way?

2. Jesus consistently refused to take shortcuts with the Father's plan for His life. We see this most clearly when Satan tempted Him in the wilderness at the beginning of His ministry, or when the crowds wanted to anoint Him king. Have you been tempted to take shortcuts in your life?

3. Jesus displayed an unhurried reliance upon His Heavenly Father. Reflect upon your own experience. When is it difficult for you to rely upon God and His timing?

4. Jesus consistently prioritized spending time with individual people over keeping a schedule. How do you handle interruptions? Are there people in your life that you need to make time for?

David Rox

13

Switchbacks: FOR YOU AND ME

Nothing is Easy. – song by Jethro Tull

And we know that in all things God works for the good of those who love him, who have been called according to his purpose. (Romans 8:28)

My Story

I thought it might be good at this time to share some of the twists and turns in my own life. Although by God's grace I have not had a terribly tumultuous journey, God has surprised me with several crooked paths – especially as I look in my own "rear view mirror."

I grew up in two different small towns in northern New Jersey, the oldest of four children. My father was a man of many gifts. During World War II he was a reconnaissance photographer in the Army and a musician who played in jazz bands as a rhythm guitarist. He actually stayed in Europe a full year after the war ended to entertain the troops staying behind. After the war he met my mom and they got married. During the baby boom, he was a professional photographer specializing in taking children's photographs. Eventually he went to work as an electrical engineer for a company that made guidance systems for rockets. As you can see, he was multitalented.

My mom had grown up in a moderately Christian home, and had responded to the gospel while a teenager. But later in life she drifted away from her faith. My younger brother and my two younger sisters, along with myself, all went to church every Sunday. But it was not a very meaningful experience for any of us.

During my pre-teen years, my father was laid off from his job when defense contract budgets were cut, so he decided to pursue his dream of owning a fast food restaurant. As I said, he was a man of many talents. This became the family business throughout the rest of my childhood. As the oldest son I worked in the place as a short order cook and car hop – no roller skates, however.

During my junior high days, the pressures of owning a business became very taxing for my dad, and he developed a severe drinking problem. It became such a problem he entered a Christian alcoholic treatment program – the Keswick Colony of Mercy in Lakehurst, New Jersey. This was really the first crisis in my young life. As the oldest son, my mother leaned heavily upon me, but I had little to offer.

Through this crisis my mother rediscovered her Christian faith. While at Keswick for three months, my father heard the gospel preached effectively and surrendered his life to Christ. Our family visited him one New Year's Eve for what they called a "Watchnight Service." For the very first time, I heard a clear message about the need to have a personal relationship with Jesus Christ – to believe in His power to forgive sins and to give Him control of my life. I experienced His grace and new life while responding to the gospel message that New Year's night.

Upon returning home, I knew I had changed, but in the months and years that followed I did not know how to grow as a young believer. I took no advantage of any real Christian fellowship and read the Bible very little. My family started to attend a more Bible-based church, and this helped me stay aware of my commitment to the Lord to a certain extent.

God used two major things in my life that helped me avoid losing my faith entirely and slipping into the complete high school mess that was the 1960's – my hard work at the family restaurant and my love and commitment to music. I had become very involved in a rock band and performed regularly as the lead singer and a trombonist in a "Chicago-type" group. I poured much of my adolescent energies into this musical project.

When it came time to go to college, I knew two things: I wanted to study music, and I wanted to go to a Christian College. Somehow, I remembered I was a Christian and I wanted to grow. When I visited Gordon College in Massachusetts in the early summer of 1972, it felt like the perfect place for me – small, rural and friendly. That fall I entered as a music performance major studying trombone.

While a freshman, many changes took place. First and foremost, I took practicing my instrument very seriously. I wanted to be the best trombonist I could be. If a day went by when I had not practiced sufficiently, or if things had not gone well in the practice room, I was miserable. And I tended to make everyone else around me miserable, too. Perhaps this drive in me came from being the firstborn in my family, and also being the first in my immediate family to ever attend college. I became quite obsessed – "married to my trombone," is how my wife would describe it years later.

But other changes also were unfolding. I had roommates who took their faith seriously and by observing their lifestyles, I was encouraged to study the Bible and pray. I attended a small church in the area as a freshman that provided me with role models in my Christian walk, and I began to grow as a Christian and a musician.

The Chair of the Music Department at Gordon College, Dr. Alton Bynum, was a godly, humble, soft-spoken Christian man who took great interest in every student in our small music department. He took me aside one day during my first semester and suggested I consider becoming a music education major instead of a performance major. He made this suggestion in his typically low-key way, but when Dr. Bynum spoke, you listened. I decided to give the music education major a try, and thus embarked on a track that has marked the rest of my adult path.

A major change in my young Christian life came my sophomore year, when I decided to attend Park Street Church in Boston. At that time, there was a vibrant college-age ministry at this historic church that emphasized discipleship, accountability in relationships, and what they called a "threefold commitment" – commitment to Christ, commitment to the Body of Christ, and commitment to the work of Christ in the world. The preaching and teaching at Park Street transformed my life and allowed me many opportunities to grow and serve. It was through the church's ministry I met my wife Margot, even though we were both students at Gordon College during the same four years.

Getting involved at Park Street Church in the college ministry caused me to devote significant time to the church activities. And this presented a problem early on for me. I was having to spend less time in the practice room with my trombone. How could I grow as a musician if I were to practice less? Over time, I realized I had to decide between being a musician who happened to be a Christian, or a Christian who happened to be a musician. With the help of God and my friends, I chose the latter. Once I began spending more time at church, the strangest thing happened. My playing got better! God was honoring my choice to follow Christ's advice in Matthew 6:33: *"But seek first his kingdom and his righteousness, and all these things will be given to you as well."*

Upon graduating with a music education degree in 1976, I took a job in the inner-city – Chelsea, Massachusetts, just north of Boston. Here I was to teach for five years as a band director and general music teacher. It was a wonderful experience. Teaching in such a setting was quite a change for a young man growing up in rural New Jersey and attending a small Christian college on Boston's lovely North Shore.

During my second year as a public-school teacher, I married Margot and we started to attend a small church in Chelsea – the First Baptist Church. It was a Southern Baptist Church supported by this denomination as a church plant of sorts. There we were able to serve the children and families in a setting completely different from that of Park Street Church in Boston. We developed deep friendships and experienced a unique love and fellowship with the people there. At this time, I was experiencing culture shock in my job, and culture shock in my church home. It was a time of stretching and growth – plenty of "switchbacks!"

Dr. Bynum stayed in touch with me during my Chelsea years, sending me a steady stream of student teachers from Gordon College. During one visit, he told me a position was opening up at my alma mater in the music department. They needed someone to direct the bands, teach music education classes and to coordinate the program. And as I said earlier, when Dr. Bynum spoke, people listened.

So, after five years at Chelsea I returned to Gordon College as a professor. I had just begun my Master's Degree at Boston University, where over the next 12 years I was to work on that degree and subsequently, a doctoral degree – all the while working full-time at Gordon. Graduate study is difficult at any time, but while working full-time at a small College, it doubled the time to complete the degrees. In some ways, these years for me were perhaps similar to Jacob's years working for his Uncle Laban.

Once again, moving from teaching music in an inner-city junior high school to being a college professor at a small Christian college was a twist in my life's path. I never dreamed I would return to teach at the college level. When you teach at a small college, you often have to be a generalist more than a specialist, and over the course of my career I taught a wide variety of musical subjects that I never thought I would.

Early on in our marriage, Margot and I discovered we were not able to have children. This was a bit of a shock to us initially, but neither of us felt a great need to adopt. We saw this as an opportunity to serve the Lord in unique ways. We had a large home and we frequently opened it up to members of the college community to live with us. When asked, *"Do you have any children?"* I would frequently reply, *"No – only 1500 of them that I can send home when I am through with them."*

We had folks over frequently – both from the College and our new church home in Hamilton, Massachusetts. Many times, students and young faculty lived with us on a short-term basis. We felt richly blessed in every way.

Because we were childless, when it came time for my musical groups to go on tour representing the College, Margot was able to come with us. Whether it was with a brass quintet, brass choir, or a larger wind ensemble, the college students were able to get to know both Margot and me "up close and personal." By God's grace, we were able to model for them what a Christian marriage might look like. The relationships with students we have toured with have been lasting ones – wonderful gifts from God in our lives.

At work, God brought a major life change at a most unexpected time during my doctoral studies. I felt led to complete my courses in educational administration, because at the time I had been appointed Chair of Gordon's music department. A doctoral degree in educational leadership seemed the most logical step to equip me to serve Him going forward.

No sooner had I completed my degree when the college administration relieved me as Chair. I was confused and devastated. But the years that followed were among the happiest and most productive of my teaching career. It seemed that my doctoral studies, although not wasted, were more part of my past than my future. In retrospect, I could see this "U-turn" was for the best. I enjoyed a 38-year career as Director of Bands, and led many different musical ensembles, along with teaching conducting.

Another significant event in my life involves my younger brother, Paul. Growing up, we were pretty much inseparable. He is 15 months younger than I, and in almost every way different from me. Whereas I was outgoing and gifted academically, Paul was quiet and struggled in school. People would often accost him with the question, *"Why can't you be like your brother?"*

Suffice it to say that many of the events that led me to become a Christian caused my brother to go in the opposite direction. Paul fell into alcoholism and isolation from the rest of our family. For a time, he even ended up in jail down in Florida. Through this experience, God finally touched him and he came to a saving knowledge of Jesus Christ. He began working in a Christian rehabilitation center in Central Florida similar to the one my father attended in New Jersey so many years before. Paul now disciples young men recovering from drug and alcohol addiction, leading them to inner healing in Christ.

During the years of my brother's struggle, the men's Bible study at my church prayed for Paul for over 25 years. One man in our study especially was concerned for Paul and faithfully prayed for him, even though he had never really met him. This friend later moved with his family to Florida, and his son fell into drug addiction. The son was finally encouraged to enroll in a rehabilitation center in central Florida. Much to my friend's surprise, he discovered his son was being mentored by my brother – that fellow

Paul that he had prayed for during those 25 long years. Only God could orchestrate such a wonderful path!

In addition, let me share briefly a little of my wife's winding career journey. To this day, she is fond of saying she still does not know what she wants to be when she grows up. Margot came to Gordon College and graduated with a Biblical Studies major. Upon graduating, she entered management training with the MacDonald's Corporation. After all, what could be more logical?

After a few years of working as a manager in this fast food chain, she became an administrative assistant for a real estate development firm, and then for a civil engineering company. After working in these fields for a few years, she took a job as an admissions counselor for a local art school. While there, she pursued her interest in visual art, and then decided to attend a school of photography. Upon graduating, Margot took a job as a corporate photographer for a major construction product company. This job evolved into working more with computers and less with a camera, and she became a graphic artist for this same company.

All this time, Margot was actively serving in our local church. Several years later, a part-time position opened up at our church and Margot became the Director of Women's Ministries. So finally, she was able to return to her roots and interests seen so clearly in her choice of her undergraduate degree. Career paths sometimes reflect few straight paths, and this certainly has been the case with my wife!

A Recent Story of Some "Switchbacks"

Even while writing this book, I experienced a perfect illustration of how God often decides to have us walk crooked paths. A few years ago, our church's senior pastor of twenty years resigned suddenly. It came as quite a shock to our congregation, and after a time of grief and self-examination as a church, Board of Elders formed a Search Committee. I was chosen to serve, and subsequently elected Chair.

Our seven-person committee was a strong and gifted one, and we decided early on not to move forward in presenting a candidate to our congregation unless we were unanimous. Work commenced – developing a church profile and job description, posting the position nationally, reading resumes, scouring church websites, listening to sermons – doing our due diligence in a thorough manner. We began the search process in an organized fashion, and over the entire time we vetted over 70 candidates. About ten months into the process, our committee had two excellent candidates that we had risen to the top of our list. Both were gifted in different ways, but it became clear that we could not reach unanimous consensus on either one. Disappointed, we moved on from them and continued our work, trusting that God would lead us to the right person.

Our search continued for several more months. Another candidate rose to the top of our list – and this time we were unanimous in our enthusiasm about his candidacy. We recommended him to our Elders (according to our church bylaws), but shortly after doing so, this candidate withdrew his candidacy. He was sensing from the Lord that our church was not a good fit for him.

This bit of news was extremely discouraging to our committee. We had been working hard for fifteen months, and two members of our committee needed to resign from the committee due to work and family pressures. It was a low point morale-wise, to be sure. Our Elders appointed two new members to our committee, and in some ways, it felt like we were starting over for a third time.

A few more months passed. We oriented our new members and began to vet a new crop of candidates. It was at this time that another single candidate rose to the top. Once again, our detailed vetting process unfolded. This time, we were sensing we had finally found our next pastor. Things were falling into place rapidly, and our committee unanimously made our recommendation to the Elders. The Elders also unanimously supported our recommendation, and this time the candidate enthusiastically accepted moving forward in our process. The Elders passed the name of our candidate on to the entire congregation.

Our next step was inviting our nominee to the church for a candidate weekend to have him preach and meet the entire congregation. We would then hold a congregational meeting to vote on calling our new pastor. But God had other plans.

Just as we were scheduling all the events of our candidate weekend, the Covid-19 crisis broke. Since our selected candidate was pastoring a church in Florida and our church is in Massachusetts, the health crisis scuttled all possibilities of bringing our candidate up for the congregation to meet and get to know him and his family in person.

To further complicate things, our church is a typical New England church – one that is not on the cutting edge of technology. Our leadership had to think creatively and learn on the fly about teleconferencing, and then communicate to the entire congregation how were planned to go forward with virtual meetings.

With God's help, we were able to arrange a wide range of online meetings with our candidate. He presented a recorded message on a chosen Sunday. We held teleconferences with church staff, officers and committee chairs from our congregation. We organized a livestreamed question and answer session open to the entire congregation. We arranged mail-in ballots so that a legitimate vote could be taken. After this arduous process, our church finally called a new senior pastor – he began to serve nearly three years after our former pastor resigned.

Looking back on this process, I never would have imagined events unfolding as they did. God's plan was not a straight path, but it was a perfect one. We found His choice for our church virtually after starting over twice.

The twists and turns in my life have not been earth-shattering, but in retrospect they were times when God was at work in hidden ways. Going through your life and looking for God's winding path can be an enlightening experience. I would recommend it to you! Take time to look back and see how God has used turning points in your life's path thus far to give you His best. It will give you confidence to see that your future is securely in His hands as well.

In Conclusion

God often does not lead us in straight paths. Setbacks, disappointments, incomprehensible events all may leave us questioning what God is doing. But our experience is normal in this fallen world. The biblical characters were aware of this reality. Writers of the psalms have given expression to these things. The early church experienced such apparent setbacks. Stephen was martyred; Saul of Tarsus ravaged the young church; and the church's survival must have looked in peril. The Apostles wrote to remind believers that God was still in complete control and working out His purposes. Zig-zagging is not the whole story; it is only the surface story.

What do you expect in life, and why do you expect it? We can learn a lot about God's purpose in our lives by looking at how He worked in the lives of others just like us.

Anyone who thinks God plans to give us straight, easy paths in life has not read the Bible. The evidence is overwhelming to the contrary. As we look at the lives of many of the biblical characters, their lives are full of twists and turns – unexpected events that often caught these ordinary but godly people completely by surprise and turned their worlds upside down. They were faced with events that complicated things, destroyed plans, shattered expectations, and raised questions about what God was doing. And yet in hindsight, we see God was in control at every step. He was not in heaven wringing His hands wondering what was going to happen next.

And yet, how often do we live our lives expecting things to go smoothly, waiting for God to hand us a "wrinkle-free" life? How often do we believe that because we love God and belong to Jesus we deserve nothing but straight pathways in life?

Where did we get this idea anyway? Not from Scripture.

No doubt this false belief is a by-product of our age. We expect instant answers and quick service at every turn of our existence. We have pain, we take a pill for quick relief. When trouble comes to us, we often react like victims instead of seeing ourselves as students in God's school of life. We whine like toddlers. The truth is that like Jesus, we are to learn obedience through what we suffer. (Hebrews 5:8)

Look at the lives of these biblical figures. Why should we expect our pilgrimage to be any different? We may speak as Jacob did when talking to Pharaoh: *"My years have been few and difficult."* (Genesis 47:9) Why do we think life is going to be easy when all the evidence points to the contrary? And how can we cope with the crooked paths God blazes along our way?

Well for starters, we can do what these biblical characters did.

Go to God

The people we have looked at did not think their worlds revolved around them. When unexpected things happened, they cried out to God. Job and Elijah complained to Him. Mary pondered things in her heart. Abraham built an altar to God, worshipped and waited. David spent time alone finding strength in the Lord his God. Moses was fortunate to talk with God face to face, as one talks with a friend.

We can read His word. Ponder the things of Scripture in our hearts. Lay out our complaints before His throne. God never turns away the lamenting heart. He may not give us the specific answers we seek, but He will give us a glimpse of His glory in His good time.

Be Patient and Wait for God's Timing

As we have seen, God moves slowly at times, and yet suddenly when His time is right. Jesus seemed to lead an unhurried ministry, and yet when it was time to die, events unfolded very quickly. Joseph languished for many years in an Egyptian prison, and yet in a moment his position was changed when Pharaoh finally called upon him. Naomi thought her bitter life was over after returning to Bethlehem, and yet in a moment Boaz entered the scene and everything changed.

We are called to be patient and wait for the Lord. Moses suffered with his people in the wilderness for 40 years. David lived for many years as a fugitive after Samuel had anointed him as a young boy. Jacob labored for Laban for his wives and flocks for 20 years. Abraham waited for 24 years for his promised son and heir. These people were patient and endured. Might God be calling us to follow a similar path?

Wait for the LORD; be strong and take heart and wait for the LORD. (Psalm 27:14)

But when the set time had fully come, God sent his Son, born of a woman, born under the law, to redeem those under the law, that we might receive adoption to sonship. (Galatians 4:4-5)

It is a dangerous thing to pray for patience, because it only comes to us in the midst of trial. But spiritual strength is found down this road. And true patience can only be found in the power of the Holy Spirit. It is the fruit of the Spirit, after all.

But the fruit of the Spirit is love, joy, peace, forbearance [patience], kindness, goodness, faithfulness, gentleness and self-control. Against such things there is no law. (Galatians 5:22-23)

Live Obediently by His Grace

Like the people of Israel in Moses' day, or David who sinned with Bathsheba, many of the crooked trails in our lives are of our own making. Years of wandering in the wilderness or family pain and suffering were a result of their sinful decisions. And we are no different. Not only can we go to God and humbly ask for forgiveness, but we can surrender in obedience to Him.

But how on earth can we as sinful people live obedient lives to God? We cannot do this in our own strength. The evidence in the Bible and in our own lives attests to this overwhelmingly. One poignant example of trying to do God's work in human strength alone can be found in the Old Testament in the book of Numbers. After the spies returned with the negative report on the Promised Land, God pronounced judgment on the people of Israel because of their faithlessness. Shortly after this, many of the people had second thoughts and decided to go conquer the land in their own strength. After Moses pronounced God's judgment on the people, he warned them against any presumptuous action:

When Moses reported this to all the Israelites, they mourned bitterly. Early the next morning they went up toward the high hill country. "We have sinned," they said. "We will go up to the place the LORD promised."

But Moses said, "why are you disobeying the LORD's command? This will not succeed! Do not go up, because the LORD is not with you. You will be defeated by your enemies., for the Amalekites and Canaanites will face you there. Because you have turned away from the LORD, he will not be with you and you will fall by the sword."

Nevertheless, in their presumption they went up toward the high hill country, though neither Moses nor the ark of the LORD's covenant moved from the camp. Then the Amalekites and Canaanites who lived in that hill country came down and attacked them and beat them down all the way to Hormah. (Numbers 14:39-45)

It was a classic case of "too little, too late." Have you ever been "beaten down" while trying to do something for God in your own strength? I have!

As the Apostle Paul taught us, we cannot live the obedient life in our own strength. But because of the finished work of Jesus Christ on our behalf we can grow in grace and live more obediently.

We know that the law is spiritual; but I am unspiritual, sold as a slave to sin. I do not understand what I do. For what I want to do I do not do, but what I hate I do. And if I do what I do not want to do, I agree that the law is good. As it is, it is no longer I myself who do it, but it is sin living in me. For I know that good itself does not dwell in me, that is, in my sinful nature. For I have the desire to do what is good, but I cannot carry it out. For I do not do the good I want to do, but the evil I do not want to do—this I keep on doing. Now if I do what I do not want to do, it is no longer I who do it, but it is sin living in me that does it.

So I find this law at work: Although I want to do good, evil is right there with me. For in my inner being I delight in God's law; but I see another law at work in me, waging war against the law of my mind and making me a prisoner of the law of sin at work within me. What a wretched man I am! Who will rescue me from this body that is subject to death? Thanks be to God, who delivers me through Jesus Christ our Lord! (Romans 7:14-25)

If we walk with Christ moment by moment, we will grow in our ability to love and obey Him. The Holy Spirit is the One who empowers us to live obediently. When we fail, we can ask forgiveness and keep pressing on.

Stay Close to Fellowship

Many of the characters we have examined drew great strength from friends and family to cope with their "zig-zag" lives. Like Ruth and Naomi, we can stay close to loved ones and other believers in times of crisis and uncertainty. David had a band of men surrounding him during his time fleeing from Saul. Paul always longed for the companionship of the men he partnered with in his ministry. Even our Lord Jesus had a band of twelve men to walk with Him. And we have the blessing of the church to help us through. It would be a great shame not to take advantage of this source of strength and encouragement.

Like Elijah, we can get into deep trouble when we believe we are all alone. I am told one of the traits of depressed people is to stay in isolation. This can be a deadly choice and one that Scripture warns against.

> *As iron sharpens iron, so one person sharpens another. (Proverbs 27:17)*
>
> *Two are better than one, because they have a good return for their labor: If either of them falls down, one can help the other up. But pity anyone who falls and has no one to help them up. Also, if two lie down together, they will keep warm. But how can one keep warm alone? Though one may be overpowered, two can defend themselves. A cord of three strands is not quickly broken. (Ecclesiastes 4:9-12)*

We are meant to function within the Body of Christ – His Church. The twists and turns of life are tough enough with a church fellowship. They are often impossible to endure without one.

Keep Going Forward and Work Hard

Hard work is a big part of what fulfilling God's plan is all about. It was God's plan for Jacob to work for his crooked Uncle Laban for twenty years. Joseph had his work cut out for him for 14 years after Pharaoh promoted him to second in command over the entire nation of Egypt. Before God revealed His ultimate plan for Ruth, she had to work tirelessly in the field gathering grain. Moses had to shepherd a stiff-necked people for forty years. God never promises an easy time. He rewards faithfulness, but our path often goes through times of toil.

I have always loved the J.B. Phillips translation of the beginning of Paul's first letter to the church in Thessalonica.

> *We are always thankful as we pray for you all, for we never forget that your faith has meant solid achievement, your love has meant hard work, and the hope that you have in our Lord Jesus Christ means sheer dogged endurance in the life that you live before God, the Father of us all. (1 Thessalonians 1:2-3)*

Switchbacks

Why do we expect life to be easy? Nothing is easy. Solid achievement. Hard work. Sheer dogged endurance. This is the pathway of blessing in God's economy.

The End of the Line

Are you looking for straight paths and an easy life? Let me break it to you: God probably has other plans for you. Don't ever think you have God figured out. He is the Divine Trailblazer, and He does not create a lot of straight paths. He often prefers to have us to climb our mountains using switchbacks – and when we finish our trek, He will get all the glory.

I have drawn insight from this prayer of a Puritan saint from past generations:

> *Help me to see that though I am in the wilderness*
> *it is not all briars and barrenness.*
> *I have bread from heaven, streams from the rock,*
> *Light by day, fire by night,*
> *Thy dwelling place and thy mercy seat.*
> *I am sometimes discouraged by the way,*
> *But though winding and trying it is safe*
> *and short.*[3]

In 1894, the British hymnwriter Arthur Campbell Ainger penned these word that contain a great truth for us:

> *God is working his purpose out, as year succeeds to year, God is working his purpose out, and the time is drawing near; Nearer and nearer draws the time, the time that shall surely be, When the earth shall be filled with the glory of God As the waters cover the sea.*

We do not walk an aimless path. God's aim is perfect. We can trust Him.

Questions for Reflection and Discussion

1. Reflect upon the "switchbacks" in your own life. What have you learned through these unexpected twists and turns? How might these past experiences prepare you for future ones?

2. Out of all the stories presented in this book, which ones have resonated with you the most? What important lessons will you hopefully carry with you on your own future journey?

3. We are called to respond to tough times in our lives in the same way godly people in the past have. Think of ways you can increase your effectiveness in the areas mentioned earlier in this chapter (Go to God; Be Patient and Wait for God's Timing; Live Obediently by His Grace; Stay Close to Fellowship; Keep Going Forward; Work Hard).

Notes

1. Bennett, Arthur. *The Valley of Vision: A Collection of Puritan Prayers and Devotions.* The Banner of Truth Trust, 1975, p. 37.

2. Lewis, C.S. *Till We Have Faces: A Myth Retold.* Harper Collins, 2012, p. 351.

3. *Valley of Vision*, p. 155

David Rox

About the Author

Dr. David W. Rox holds degrees in music education from Gordon College and Boston University. He is a retired Professor of Music from Gordon College in Wenham, Massachusetts, where he taught for 38 years. He is a long-time church lay leader, Bible teacher and musician.

As a professional musician, he has conducted many instrumental ensembles including the Gordon College Wind Ensemble, Brass Quintet, Symphonic Band and Jazz Ensemble. As a college professor he also taught conducting, trombone, and courses in music education. As a trombonist he has performed with well-known artists such as The Gene Krupa Band, Rosemary Clooney, Red Buttons, Pearl Bailey, Louis Bellson, Margaret Whiting, Rose Marie, and many others. He has led ensembles throughout Europe and the United States, including important venues in Boston, Quebec, Paris, London, Rome, Florence, Cannes and Dublin. He has served as President of the New England College Band Association and appears frequently as guest conductor, adjudicator and clinician for school festivals. He and his wife Margot live in Rowley, Massachusetts.

For more information contact:

>Dr. David Rox
>C/O Advantage Books
>info@advbooks.com

To purchase additional copies of these books, visit our bookstore at www.advbookstore.com

>Orlando, Florida, USA
>"we bring dreams to life"™
>www.advbookstore.com

www.ingramcontent.com/pod-product-compliance
Lightning Source LLC
Chambersburg PA
CBHW050801160426
43192CB00010B/1594